SO YOUR CHILD IS A COMPLETE ARSEHOLE

Becci Abbott

SO YOUR CHILD IS A COMPLETE ARSEHOLE

First published in Great Britain as a softback original in 2020

Copyright © Becci Abbott

The moral right of this author has been asserted.

All rights reserved.

No part of this publication may be reproduced, stored in a retrieval system, or transmitted, in any form or by any means, without the prior permission in writing of the publisher, nor be otherwise circulated in any form of binding or cover other than that in which it is published and without a similar condition including this condition being imposed on the subsequent purchaser.

Typeset in Athelas

Editing, design, typesetting and publishing by UK Book Publishing

www.ukbookpublishing.com

ISBN: 978-1-913179-74-8

Contents

Introduction _____ 1

PART 1: The Early Years

My big brother _____ 7

The time mum was very successful in introducing me to ballet _____ 9

The first time mum and dad let me pack my own suitcase _____ 10

The time I was an entrepreneur _____ 12

The time my aunty was in labour _____ 15

The time I met my uncle's new girlfriend and really
really liked her _____ 16

The time I ran away _____ 18

The time I played teacher _____ 20

PART 2: The Teenager

The transition _____ 24

All those times I didn't want to go on a bloody walk _____ 28

The time I completely ruined my bedroom walls _____ 31

The time I didn't see Shrek 3 _____ 32

The emo phase _____ 34

The times Dad said I couldn't have friends over _____ 38

CONTENTS

The times I would get really really mad — 39

The time I had my 16th birthday party — 41

The time my cousin and I hotboxed a wendy house — 47

The time my teacher called me a part-timer — 49

The times I didn't understand why Mum is so sensitive — 51

The time we played 'lights' — 53

BONUS STORY: The time Dad thought it would be funny to newspaper over my doorway while I was asleep — 55

The time I made that bad decision — 57

The times we were disturbed by our neighbour — 58

The 'S' word — 60

The time we went to the underpass — 65

The time we snuck onto the sports field — 72

The house on Wellesley Avenue — 74

The time I was a layabout — 76

The time we had a bonfire in the garden — 79

BONUS STORY: The time I was extremely confused — 80

The time we saw that evening standard article — 82

The time I got a tattoo — 86

The time it got better — 89

The male parental unit — 93

The female parental unit — 101

Acknowledgements — 110

Julie — 117

About the Author — **127**

*Dedicated to Mum and Dad.
Obviously.*

To Ruth, Jay & the rest of the team at UK Book Publishing, words can't express my gratitude. You took my scrappy little idea and made it real. Thank you for your kindness, your patience and your dedication. Thank you for all you do and for printing the words of this arsehole for all the other arseholes out there. I'm sure they're just as grateful as me.

Introduction

This is not a 'How To' book.

In fact this is really really really really definitely and categorically not a 'How To' book. I wouldn't dare act as though I have any right to suggest 'How To' do anything really. I'd be more help writing a book on how to carve a banana so it looks ever so slightly like Lily Allen than I would on writing a practical guide to parenting.

In this book you'll find no useful tips or diagrams or resources or suggestions (aside from the odd checklist or two). What you will find is a series of real, genuine little moments from across my childhood, some with my thoughts looking back on them now, but most just as they are. No excuses, just little honest pieces of shittery from my shittest period. Here for you, dear reader, to enjoy. You don't even need to read them chronologically if you're feeling especially saucy; whenever you're having a bad day or a particularly awful argument, feel free to pick this book up at whatever point and read one of the little stories and hopefully you'll think, 'well my situation is bad but at least it's not Becci Abbott's parents bad'.

Perhaps you are the parent of an, erm, 'vivacious' child or stroppy teenager and want to know it's not your fault. If this is the case, I promise you, it's not your fault.

Perhaps you are now or once were, like me, an emotionally volatile, painfully uncool and generally angry teenager for no justifiable reason and it would feel nice to know you're not alone and you're not an awful person. If this is you, I promise you, you might have been a little bit awful at times but you're not an awful person and you're definitely not alone.

Perhaps you're actually none of these things and picked up this book by mistake somehow tricked into believing it might be a book about something interesting and fun, perhaps even porn, and just now that you're reading this sentence you're realising that you've made a grave mistake. If this is you... well, soz. It's not porn nor is it fun. But, seeing as how you're here anyway... welcome, disappointed stranger.

Whichever one of these categories you fall into (or if you're none of the above), I hope this book offers you all something positive, whatever it may be. Being a teenager is hard (no joke it is really, really fucking hard); being the parent of one is even harder. This book won't offer any solutions – I wouldn't dare pretend I have the right to suggest any – but I at least hope that my brutally honest and shameful accounts of actual experiences from mine and my parents' lives whilst I was growing up give you something nice for a moment. Maybe one will make you smile for a second. You might cruelly laugh with mirth. You might feel really smug that you're a perfect parent of a perfect child and will never have to experience what we did. Or, maybe, you'll disagree entirely with everything I say and the way I said it and get really angry at what a chuffing well waste of money this is and storm off instead to go and write your own book that you DO like (maybe some porn?), which of course would be excellent for you and I actively encourage and celebrate your creative endeavours.

What about my relationship with my parents now? Well, due to their incalculable patience and strength of forgiveness I now have a wonderful and very close relationship with them and am lucky enough to be able to speak to them almost every day (mostly via Skype given they're still down in London and I'm up in Glasgow). My worst years are now somewhat of a funny anecdote in my house, mostly revived in the form of ammo used by my mum to win arguments.

Mum and Dad really are very special people for lots of reasons. They've welcomed my friends into our family in a very real sense and we all spend a lot of time together due to our shared love of card / board / online gaming, and it took me a while but I finally became appreciative of everything they did for me. In truth, I'm quite honoured to have been raised by such incredibly kind, funny and patient people. It took me a little while to finally drag myself out of my teenage idiocy and appreciate them, but I got there eventually.

My parents went through an awful lot of crap when I was in my awkward teenage years that I wish I could take back, but I can't. It all happened. But maybe what I *can* do in their honour is tell you, my dear reader, some of our stories and then maybe...just maybe... someone will relate. And maybe... just maybe... they might forgive me.

Maybe.

A note before we start

Before we begin, a note to you, my lovely reader. Therein lies the exact issue; I don't like not being able to address you personally. This is a very personal little book so I feel like we should address each other with more familiarity than just 'Reader', don't you think? And given it would take me far too long to research all your individual names then print and send you your own special copy of the book with your name in – by which point you probably would have lost the small spark of interest you had in wanting to read this book in the first place and gone and bought another book instead, so I really don't have the time nor the money for such a fruitless endeavour, what a stupid suggestion – I will instead refer to you as 'Stan'. It will make it easier for me to address you in this book as I would a close friend or confidant. So, from hereon in, whenever I refer to 'Stan' at any point in this book, please understand that I am addressing you personally and specifically. Gender, age, religion, sexual orientation, zodiac sign, actual name and politics aside. You are Stan now. So, whenever I say 'Stan', please believe that it's you I'm talking to, genuinely and whole-heartedly. And if your name is actually Stan and you've decided to ignore this section then you're about to be rather confused.

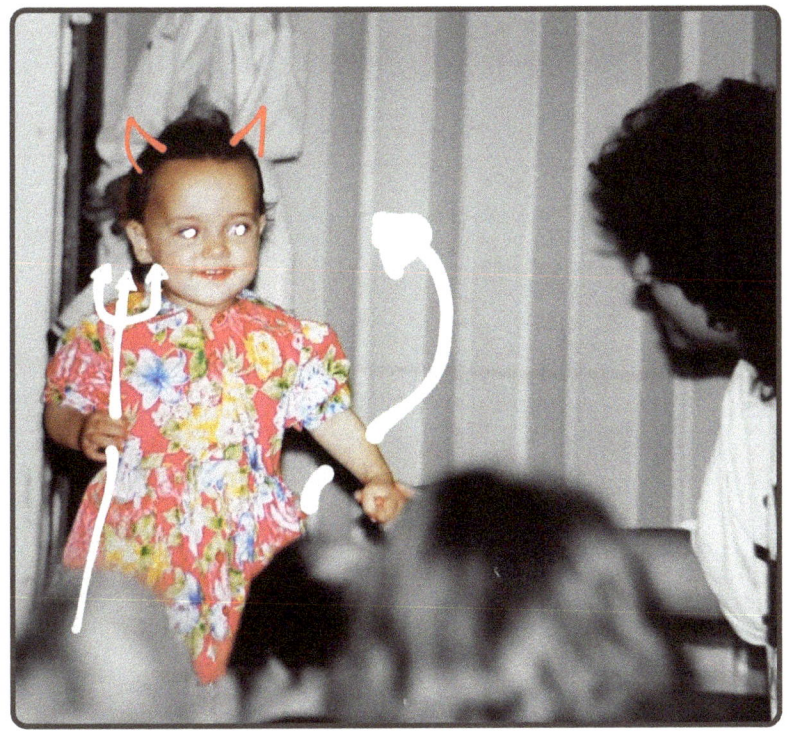

PART 1
The Early Years

(AKA THE WARM UP)

BECCI ABBOTT

My big brother

TWATTERY SCORE: 9/10

Jamie, Jamie, Jamie.

Oh, the stories that could be told about the arguments caused by, or had with, my PeRfEcT big brother Jamie. I could probably write a whole book on this topic alone (but I wouldn't do that to you, Stan, because that would be really boring).

I won't go into any specific circumstances but it's important contextually to understand that my brother burst forth into the world in 1991, a gloriously sweet, innocent and endlessly happy bouncing baby boy that changed my parents' worlds for the better. I've always said that Jamie is so irritatingly cheerful all the time that he farts rainbows. He goes through life (still even now) as a happy, fluffy beam of energetic sunshine with brightly coloured hair.

Then I happened.

My parents' previous conception of having a baby had until that point been easy breezy, even to the point that they thought, 'Jesus, what's all the fuss about? Parenting's a doddle!'.

SO YOUR CHILD IS A COMPLETE ARSEHOLE

Needless to say that my parents got the shock of their lives when, two and a bit years later, out of my mother crawled a screeching, squealing, painfully loud and constantly crying, fat, angry little baby-shaped attention-seeking missile, sent forth from below solely to ruin my parents' lives.

Mum loved to say to me that if I'd have come first, they'd have never had a second child. Thanks, Mum.

Rather conveniently, soon after my birth was when my Dad tactfully decided he "doesn't do babies" and so spent these initial years of my life playing football with the fun one, whilst Mum tried to figure out why the annoying one was screaming *this* time (usually boredom). In Dad's position I like to think I'd do the same.

Even now they refer to Jamie as 'first born and favourite'. I mean, after some of the stuff you'll read in this book, I don't think anyone would blame them.

The time mum was very successful in introducing me to ballet

TWATTERY SCORE: 5/10

I was, I think, five or six. Mum put me in a little pink tutu over a purple leotard (which, by the way, I thought was magnificent) and took me to a ballet class where I was the youngest attendee by far. I think she thought it would be nice to give me the perfect opportunity to perhaps inherit a little bit of poise, grace and dignity from my older classmates.

What in fact happened was that I thought it would be far more interesting instead to spend the hour shooting up and down the hall, careering from one end of the room to the other like a crazed little rocket full of nonsense and wearing a tiny tutu.

Mum never took me back to ballet.

SO YOUR CHILD IS A COMPLETE ARSEHOLE

The first time mum and dad let me pack my own suitcase

TWATTERY SCORE: 6.1/10

It was Winter. 1999. I must have been around six.

Mum, Dad, my brother Jamie and I were due to go on a wintery holiday to Devon where my grandparents lived.

Being the precocious little gobshite that I am, I somehow managed to convince my parents that I was grown up enough to pack my own suitcase for the holiday, that I'm not a baby any more, to please let me try.

Impressed with this shining confidence and maturity, Mum and Dad clearly thought wow, ok, yeah amazing, you go for it, girl. What a smart little angel our baby is.

We got to my grandparents' house in Devon after a few hours' drive and Mum helped me unpack. Upon doing so she discovers that her smart little angel took it upon herself in all her new-found adulthood to pack absolutely buggering nothing for the winter holiday except for three summer dresses and a fairy outfit.

Mum and Dad, embarrassed, had to take me to the shops to get me winter clothes and some pants (as I'd packed none). Score.

SO YOUR CHILD IS A COMPLETE ARSEHOLE

The time I was an entrepreneur

TWATTERY SCORE: 7.5/10

I think we all reach a point in our childhood where we go from not giving a flying fig about money (because as far as we're concerned 'money' is just a word that makes Mummy and Daddy fight a lot and we would much rather play 'how many times can I hit my brother with this plastic double-ended Darth Maul lightsaber before he tells on me') to realising that money can actually be exchanged in shops for goods and services. And once we realise this then, suddenly we care about money. We care quite a lot.

This point came for me at around the age of seven or eight. That light switched in my head as it does with us at all one point and the growing hunger for money began.

My fascination and desperation for dat sweet, sweet dolla soon monstered out of proportion and overtook my better judgement, to the extent that at a certain point on a semi-regular basis I would quietly tiptoe down the stairs after I was meant to be asleep, slowly pull my dad's wallet out of his coat pocket and slip a few 10ps – or maybe even a 50p if I was feeling frisky – into my little hand. I'd then softly softly gently gently creep back upstairs to proudly and gleefully count my stolen riches (which to me really were riches), somewhat akin to Smaug in Lord of the Rings sitting greedily on top of his pile of treasure. Looking back on it now, I'm of course very ashamed to admit this, and Dad, if you're reading this, I'm really sorry.

However, the glee was short-lived. Soon realising that stealing is wrong and starting to feel overcome with guilt, I came up with a much better plan. Rather than stealing money (bad) I'd just steal items from around the house and then sell them back to Mum and Dad (very good). I know, bloody genius, isn't it?

My shiny new plan involved collecting random items from around the house that Mum and Dad already owned, display them on a little red plastic table on the landing outside my bedroom with little handwritten prices Sellotaped to each (Mum's ruler 10p, Dad's stapler 30p, TV remote £1, etc.). I even had a little makeshift till that I fashioned out of some old cereal boxes.

Mum and Dad, being the sweet and supportive parents that they are, played along with this façade for a little while – probably happy I'd stopped the wallet stealing which they absolutely knew about (it turns out 7-or-8-year-olds aren't as sneaky as they think they are) – and bought some items back off me. I remember very, very clearly being so very proud of 7-year-old-self for coming up with such a clearly brilliant plan which I couldn't believe no-one had thought of before, and I would daydream about how I would eventually expand my enterprise so would probably need to invest in (steal) a bigger table so I could fit the TV on, and I wondered if I could get the cat to stay still for that long.

I was certain I would be able to make money forever and I'd be the brilliantly rich grown-up running a successful shop from my childhood landing. I could not fathom that this wasn't a solid business model.

Alas, sadly, it wasn't long before Mum and Dad got bored of playing along with this little game, which was essentially based off of them paying twice for their own stuff, and so shortly thereafter its creation, Becci's Little Shop of Horrors, was eventually, to my despair, made insolvent.

I've got to hand it to myself though, it's as Murphy's Law of Combat states: If it's stupid but it works then it's not stupid.

BECCI ABBOTT

The time my aunty was in labour

TWATTERY SCORE: 666/10

I must've been around eight. My aunty was in hospital in labour. Her two other younger children (my little cousins) were staying with us during this period.

Of course being the protective, smarter and wiser older cousin that I was, I took it upon myself to put my comforting arm around her youngest child, my baby cousin (4), and tell her, helpfully, reassuringly: 'By the way, your mum is dead'.

She wasn't dead. She was far from dead (if there's such a thing as being far from dead, like being alive, for instance?). No-one had told me she was dead. Why and from where I decided to spout this helpful information I honestly have absolutely no idea. I don't *think* this was done out of malice, but just me being a total idiot and doing a Young Becci Special of relaying opinion (or altogether made-up information) confidently as though it's fact. This occasion was, of course, met with great distress.

My uncle was thrilled.

SO YOUR CHILD IS A COMPLETE ARSEHOLE

The time I met my uncle's new girlfriend and really really liked her

TWATTERY SCORE: 9/10

It was 1998 and I was five (a strong year for me).

My Uncle John says: 'Becci, this is Molly*'.

Me, having climbed onto the arm of the sofa so that I could get to eye level with this new stranger:

'You can go home now, lady.'

*Not her real name

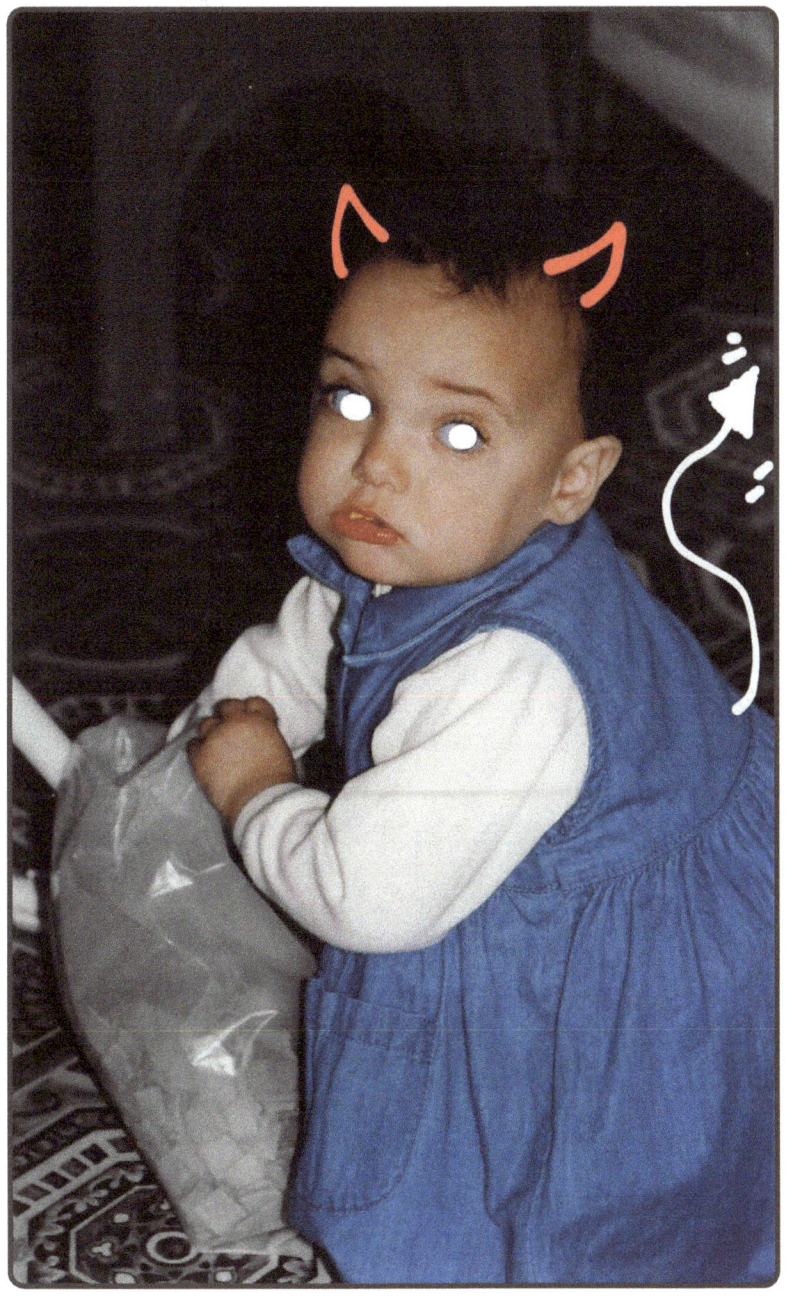

The time I ran away

TWATTERY SCORE: 7.5/10

When I was about seven I had, as per, a big bust up with Mum and Dad. Hurt, angry and ever the thespian, I decided that it was time to teach them a lesson and do that movie classic: I would run away. That would show them. I'd pack a tablecloth full of my belongings tied to the end of a stick like they do in Pingu and run away never to return. Then – THEN they'd be sorry for being so horrible to me (they'd probably asked me to take a bath or something equally mundane). Oh, they would cry and they would shout and they would fall to their knees and cry out: 'WHY WAS I SO HORRIBLE TO MY PERFECT LITTLE GIRL?!'

And this is almost precisely the devastating effect that my running away had. I did actually pack my things up (my favourite clip-on earrings and a toy lightsaber) into a little tablecloth like I said I would (although I had to ditch the stick because there was no time to find a suitable one) and I did actually leave the house. I ran away.

Unfortunately, being only seven and having no real understanding of travel, distance or any common sense whatsoever, my running away amounted to me walking out of the front door, down the front path and then standing six metres away from the house by our own hedge. Not even next door's hedge or the hedge one further house down; I'd "run away" so successfully that I was still beside our own stupid bloody hedge. I was still on our own property. They could still see me out of the window.

As soon as it became apparent that no-one cared about my dramatic escape and nor was anyone following me, I promptly did the walk of shame back into the house.

Parents 1 - 0 Becci.

From Left: Jamie, Cousin, Satan Herself, Cousin.

SO YOUR CHILD IS A COMPLETE ARSEHOLE

The time I played teacher

TWATTERY SCORE: 6.8/10

I used to LOVE playing schoolteacher when I was little. Being naturally bossy, the opportunity to boss other kids around and show that I was the more mature, wise, important one was a total joy. It's a game I used to force my poor little cousins Louise and Emily to play with me, both of whom would generally oblige for the most part until they got bored or I was too mean and they'd run off crying (sorry, girls, not my fault; I don't make the rules of this game I just made up).

I remember having little fuzzy animal stickers that came with a magazine I'd read, and I'd use them to grade my cousins' homework and used my bedroom wall as a sticker chart to track their progress.

Looking back now, if I could, I would pay hard cash for the chance to see the work I gave them to do at the time, as one can only imagine what the brain of an eight year old puts together as classroom tasks and work. What a fun game that must have been for them. I only remember there being plastic folders full of copied sheets and lined paper but I think I also just liked photocopying and pretending to do general office stuff which I considered to be the height of sophistication, so they were probably photocopies of nothing.

I remember that at one point I used our family computer (remember that? A world where there was just the one shared family computer?) to type up letters to the parents of my cousins and then went downstairs to the kitchen (it must have been a family birthday and everyone was over) and asked my aunts and uncles to sign them. These letters would agree for said aunts and uncles to essentially sign over the girls' education to me and promise to withdraw them from school as they would be taught by me at my boarding school from now on.

I also remember how genuinely very, very, very confused I was when the parents then took the girls home later that day. I didn't understand why they were taking them away when they were enrolled in my school. This was before distance learning was a thing as well, so at the time I thought it somewhat impractical for the parents to take my students away the day before their first official induction day just to have to drive them all the way back over to our house for their first day of their new school (my bedroom) the following day, but grown-ups aren't very smart sometimes.

Needless to say, I eventually figured out that their parents had almost no interest in withdrawing their kids from full-time education. No wonder they turned out so terribly.

SO YOUR CHILD IS A COMPLETE ARSEHOLE

PART 2
The Teenager

SO YOUR CHILD IS A COMPLETE ARSEHOLE

The transition

TWATTERY SCORE: 8.8/10

It's quite an experience really, making the leap from primary to secondary school. One day you're in year 6 and your main focus in life is making sure you get to the rope swing on the playground first, or getting those multi-coloured thread braid things on holiday and impressing all your mates, or what you'll do during the school holidays. Also, party bags at friend's birthday parties – how fun were they?

School work is easy, teachers love you and you're totally in control. Everything's happy and sweet and brilliant.

The next second you're in your first day of secondary school. You place one little brand-new-shiny-black-shoed foot on the school grounds and before you know it you get a lit cigarette thrust forcefully in one hand, a bottle of vodka pressed into the other and people whisper about blowjobs in your ear, before patting you on the back, pushing you forcefully into your teenage experience and leaving you to it to see what happens (after the same is done to all the other 110 kids in your year too). Innocent little you is shocked and confused in your little blazer that's way too big for you. It's really, really scary and new and adult and full of rule-breaking and trying stuff and emotions you don't understand. It's incredible really how quickly the primary school innocence is dissolved, and life starts beating you in the face with a pressure mallet.

Everyone starts looking at each other (really, really looking at each other) and cliques and groups and judgement and jealousy and bitching and gossiping starts. It's not done out of cruelty most of the time, it's usually done because everyone doesn't want the attention on them and wants to feel like one of the normal ones. They know that the tide will turn any second and then people will be talking about the spot on *their* chin or their cold sore or their stupid haircut or their sudden weight gain, so they divert the attention. Not even in any conscious way, but that's what they're doing even if they don't realise it.

Also, think about it: at school you sit around a foot away from all the other desks. Think about that for a second. A classroom of 30 horny, emotional, bored, slightly vicious and self-conscious kids, all sat within reaching distance and able to see each other's faces really closely in high detail. All day. Every day. Would you want to sit on a desk a foot away in every direction from a bunch of 12 and 13-year-old kids right now staring at your face and judging you? I didn't think so. It's an intense and closely packed situation and it's no wonder it leads to all sorts of drama and self-hatred. At least when you're an adult, office desks are a relatively respectable size and distance away from other people (that obviously doesn't apply to a lot of jobs that aren't office-based but you get my point). Perhaps in a post-COVID-19 world this pressure will be eased slightly as kids are spaced further apart for hygiene reasons, but social distancing won't save us from my next point:

Hormones. Hormones are a right fucker. Just to totally spitball off the top of my head, **A hormone** (from the Greek participle ὁρμῶν, "setting in motion") is any member of a class of signalling molecules, produced by glands in multicellular organisms, that are transported by the circulatory system to target distant organs to regulate physiology and behaviour[1], but that's just my personal opinion.

Basically, hormones signal the turning point from kidulthood to adulthood (and while we're at it, the films of the same name were excellent) and I'm sure we can all agree are probably the foundations upon which teenage arseholery is built, whether visible (hello spots) or invisible (in the form of pure, boiling rage lava).

In my case, the main emotion introduced into my life as an early teenager as part of my glorious teenage hormonal package and which, to be honest, has never quite fully left, was the sads. Sads in the form of unnecessarily overdramatic melancholy, self-hatred and general annoyance at myself for not thinking I was fitting in; none of this helped by the onset of periods, spots, being awkwardly uncool, a gap tooth you could twirl a baton between and suddenly growing boobs that make you look like you're smuggling two ripe cantaloupes inside a turtle neck and having absolutely no bloody clue what to do with them.

The early teenage years are super intense as, in addition to everything I've outlined above, this is when we start to become sexualised (see aforementioned bit about cantaloupes), social media accounts start to become commonplace and a Kilimanjaro-sized mountain of pressure to look good gets heaped onto our shoulders. Add this on top of starting to form your personality and long-term friendships, schoolwork, choosing your future career-path pressures and those pesky hormones I was talking about, and you have yourself a whirling vortex of emotion. For some teenagers this might come out in the form of art or sports or wanking or drinking, but in my case, it spilled out in the grizzly form of the uncontrollable rage beast.

The point is, this inherent teenage narcissism was probably the crux of most of the tensions, crossed wires and frictions in the relationship between myself and my parents. There were so many things happening in my life that a whole stream of brand-new and complex dynamics, instincts and emotions had burst out of my once-innocent (well...ish) youthful seams and spilled, messily, confusingly, onto my lap, and therefore by proximity also onto the laps of my parents. There was no room to think or even care about their feelings.

Hello world, the most important person in existence has arrived.

---

[1] https://en.wikipedia.org/wiki/Hormone

SO YOUR CHILD IS A COMPLETE ARSEHOLE

All those times I didn't want to go on a bloody walk

TWATTERY SCORE: 9.1/10

This was one of the sorest and most frequent sources of friction in our house. Mum would constantly ask me to go on a walk with her, in her mind wanting to give us a chance to connect in the same way she did with her mum.

In my mind, rather than accepting that Mum was just wanting to spend some quality time with me, I was convinced that she and her other Mum friends secretly met up and giggled and plotted how many ridiculous ways that they could interrupt their children's exponentially busy schedules with pointless and meaningless tasks, for no reason other than spite. To me, she may as well have been asking me to take a feather duster to her rhododendrons just for shits and giggles.

What Mum wasn't to know (because I never told her anything) is that there was usually something far more fascinating going on on my computer that I simply couldn't tear myself away from, such as, for example, building my Piczo website, blending photoshoot images of Lindsay Lohan together with Photoshop (for purposes that I honestly cannot fathom now but somehow seemed very important at the time), sending 'Luv' on Bebo, or that I'd been flirting with my cousin's mate Tom on Facebook for almost a week so knew he'd probably ask me out soon, which had meant I'd been busy coming up with witty and sarcastic Tweets because I knew he followed me on Twitter but I was pretending I didn't know he did and this way he'd know how utterly naturally fascinating I was and how bothered by him I wasn't. Not to mention the fact that my main Sim had just had an affair and gotten the maid pregnant, so things were really getting juicy in that department. So, no Mum, I'll pass on your 'walk', thanks.

The more Mum would ask me to go on a walk with her the more frustrated I would get, and as an automatic unavoidable physical reaction I would dig in my heels and the familiar traits of laziness and stubbornness would kick into action. Whenever she would ask me, I couldn't think of anything I wanted to do less then get up out of my chair. I don't think I can overexaggerate how deep my lazy and stubborn instincts are (my cup runneth over), so whenever she asked me I genuinely, honestly, really couldn't muster up the energy. You know that way that once you know you really should do something (get up early, go for a run, take the bins out), suddenly your body makes it physically impossible to do so? Yeah, that.

This argument happened so frequently that it got to the point that even before I'd had a chance to respond to the offer of a walk, Mum would already be somewhat snarkily defensive, though who could blame her. I'd ask her to give me 10 minutes, or sigh in a way that she deemed to be disinterested and she'd say "fine, whatever" and storm out of the house. I mean, she wasn't wrong; 10 minutes usually turned into 45 minutes which became two hours which became never, and yes, I actually was sighing with disinterest.

We sometimes go on walks now. They're nice.

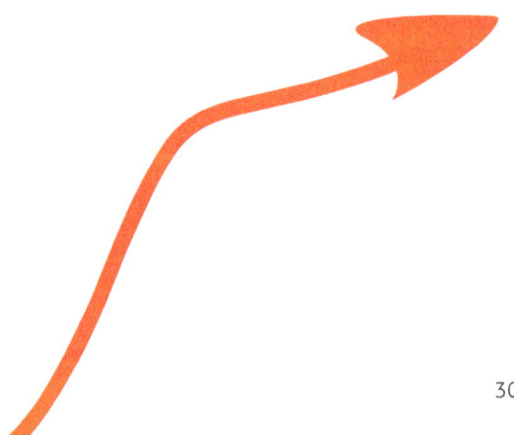

BECCI ABBOTT

The time I completely ruined my bedroom walls

TWATTERY SCORE: 8.4/10

My friend K adding in some finishing touches. If you think this is bad; it got worse.

SO YOUR CHILD IS A COMPLETE ARSEHOLE

The time I didn't see Shrek 3

TWATTERY SCORE: 9.4/10

I was 14 and in year 8 of secondary school and half term was about to start. My surprisingly long-term boyfriend of eight months (for any grown-ups who don't know or have forgotten, dating for eight months in school is basically the equivalent of 40 years of marriage when you're 14) and I were due to go to Slough cinema with two of our friends. As it was the last day before half term, the school finished early at 1pm, just after lunch.

My then-husband-boyfriend, we'll just call him S, had a brilliant idea. He remembered that he had leftover wine in his locker that his mum gave him for the school raffle, and he'd forgotten to hand them in, so why don't we bring them to the cinema and drink them? We're adults now and adults drink wine.

What an absolutely fool-proof, sensible and risk-free idea that was.

Giddy with excitement and utterly confident with what a smashing idea we'd had, we snuck the wine bottles – three red and one white, so classy – into our school bags and sauntered off to see Shrek 3 (it baffles me too that I could have been as old as 14 when that movie came out).

I woke up later that evening in Queensmere Shopping Centre public toilets where I'd been slumped unconscious over a toilet bowl – having vomited profusely – with my school friend Joe's mum gently shaking me awake as she'd found me in there, slumped but still clutching a loaf of bread in my hand that I'd apparently bought earlier in a drunken stupor. There was a crowd behind her of Queensmere Shopping Centre security staff and some paramedics. Not a sight that you forget easily, Stan, I can tell you.

We were subsequently barred from Slough Cinema, which really is quite a low point, though of course this is impossible to enforce so naturally we went back many times after.

I was fine, I just had to be shamefully picked up by Mum and proceeded to throw up a lot. Poor S ended up in hospital (he'd been found apparently unconscious after spending 20 minutes shouting at his own reflection in the window of Toni & Guy) and had to get his stomach pumped.

On the bright side, we look back on this incident somewhat fondly as it meant I learned my limits very early on in my teenage years and didn't touch wine for many years after.

Thank you for your kindness that day, Joe's mum.

The emo phase

TWATTERY SCORE: 8.5/10

I went through the 'emo' phase that was popular for a few years in the early 00s with absolute gusto. The beauty of this movement was that we could pretend that not fitting in and being weird was a conscious choice rather than an unfortunate side-effect; hence its widespread appeal.

For those who don't recall the emo phase or were actually cool as teenagers so don't have a clue what being an 'emo' entails, fear not!! I've compiled a handy checklist just for you guys to send you well on your way to being an excellent emo and utterly terrorise those around you (I can send laminated versions of these lists on request):

- Eyeliner. Sooooo much eyeliner.
- Spend roughly 45-55 minutes back-combing your hair and using lots of extra-strength hairspray so it's nice and stiff and messy and shows people you put no effort in.
- If your hair is long enough, make sure your fringe lies at a strict horizontal angle over your face from the top of one ear to the top of the other, even if it's really unnatural and looks really weird and takes ages

to force to stay in that position. Trust me, you look amazing. Ideally, cut your own fringe.
- Wear checkered braces hanging down off your purple superskinny jeans.
- Get Converse or Vans (ideally with flames on the side but checkered black or white ones are also fine if the flame ones are sold out).
- Teachers and parents don't get you. No-one gets you; you're deeper, cooler and artsier than they are. Bottle that and use that to write terrible poetry.
- Get yourself accustomed to photoshop; you'll need it. Every selfie from now on is in black and white; don't be afraid to add cool black rectangles over your eyes and scribbles over your mouth to show people that you're incredibly deep, artsy and creative because otherwise they won't know.
- Slam all the doors. If you don't have many doors to slam, you'll have to find some in other rooms or buildings and slam those.
- Feel all the emotions (and make it known, usually by telling people). I mean that's what 'emo' is short for anyway, so you feel free to feel everything, you glorious, sensitive baby.
- If you've got any of those tennis sweatbands in black, they make a great fashion accessory with every outfit. If not, then your mum's blue Nike ones will do.
- Doodle lyrics everywhere. Your schoolbooks, your arms (FYI this also makes for a good dramatic Bebo profile pic), your pets etc.

- If you end up finding yourself accidentally cheerful one day, never fear; just listen to a bit of Hawthorne Heights or Bullet For My Valentine on your camouflage-decorated Walkman and it'll bring you back down again.
- Speaking of Hawthorne Heights, you're so into music. I mean like so, so into music. Music gets you like people don't. Embrace this and listen to the angriest, screamiest or saddest music as loud as possible and feel all the things. Try and find the most obscure band possible (even if they're complete and utter shit) by reading rubbish music blogs and write the band name or song lyrics anywhere that people might see, in order to pretend you like the band and to prove to everyone that you're just way more into music than they are.
- Put initials of the person you have a crush on in your MSN status (for any current teenagers, the equivalent nowadays would be in your WhatsApp status, or your TikTok…? I don't bloody know) with heart emojis either side. This way they'll hopefully notice and you can just pretend they're someone else's initials if they don't like you back.
- Buy a baggy, really really really oversized and pretty disgusting brown men's XXXL jumper from Primark that doesn't suit you at all. Wear this to your school mufty (own clothes) day and make sure to hang out and nonchalantly in your form room with your other emo friends whilst everyone's outside to show that you don't conform and the school system can't contain you (but otherwise follow all the rules and do everything the

teachers say of course so you don't get in trouble cause you're an emo 'til you die but education is important).
- Black, white or pink (or one of each) plastic bead necklaces are a solid move.
- Wearing animal ears / super bright clothing / boy's comic graphic print boxers over your skinny jeans "ironically".
- Make sure you have some deep problems. If your life isn't that bad and your parents are wankers who genuinely love and support you like mine did, create drama by being really rude to them for no reason. This will force them to shout at you and punish you so then you get to feel bad about that and write about it on your blog (or if it's 2005, your Piczo website).
- Whenever someone says, 'it's a phase', roll your eyes and scoff. What they don't know is that you'll be like this forever (you won't be like it forever and you'll get bored of it when it stops being popular in a couple of months, but you don't know that yet).

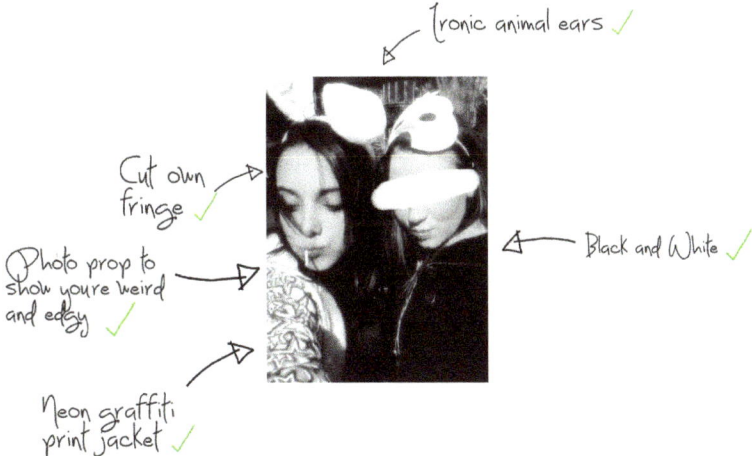

Ironic animal ears ✓

Cut own fringe ✓

Photo prop to show you're weird and edgy ✓

Black and White ✓

Neon graffiti print jacket ✓

SO YOUR CHILD IS A COMPLETE ARSEHOLE

The times Dad said I couldn't have friends over

TWATTERY SCORE: 9/10

I would just have them over anyway.

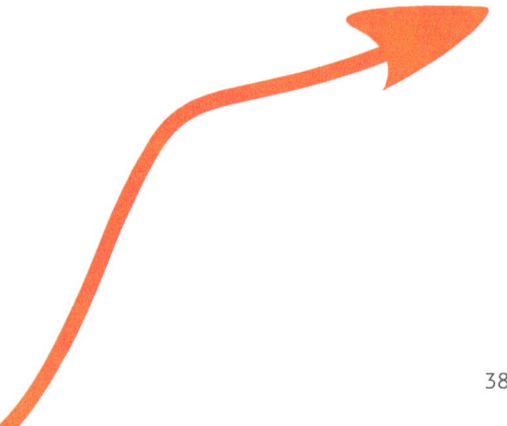

The times I would get really really mad

TWATTERY SCORE: 9.9/10

Ok, I admit it, I probably have an anger problem. I know, I bet I could blow you over with a feather at that piece of startling information.

My constant anger was especially prevalent whilst I was a teenager living at home as my anger wasn't always necessarily tied down to anything; just general fury and never really feeling happy with myself. I hated not being one of the pretty ones in my school and having to shave my top lip which was sooooo embarrassing, and I hated always having an old phone because we couldn't afford the fancy brand new Motorola Razr that loads of the cool girls in school had, and none of the boys fancied me and everyone in school probably laughed about me whenever I walked in a room.

One of my biggest shames (and it really pains me to admit this on paper) was that I would constantly lash out at Mum and Dad so very unfairly. Mostly it would be when they disturbed me as all I ever wanted was to be on my own. A teenager's relationship with their phone and computer is an all-encompassing thing, especially as usually we'll be talking to mates or, worst of all, our crushes, and when you're getting hot & heavy or exploring new, weird, confusing feelings (more on this later), you really don't want to be playing cards with your dad and your brother, or having your mum come into your room asking you to take the bins out, or to be honest having any reminder of the fact that they're anywhere within even the same postcode as you. You really, really don't want them around, but you have no choice.

On certain occasions Mum would innocently come in my room while I was getting changed, and (don't hate me, Stan) I'd scream at her for barging in, calling her a perv and all sorts of other awful things that I really wish I didn't have to type. I also had a habit of trashing my room whenever I was annoyed at my parents or myself; smashing things and breaking stuff I loved. At the time I didn't know why I was getting angry nor did I really realise how closely the anger was tied to my self-hatred, but all I knew was that everything was shit and my parents wouldn't leave me alone.

I get this gene from my Dad as he has been known to throw the odd steak and kidney pie against the kitchen wall during a shouting match.

The time I had my 16th birthday party

TWATTERY SCORE: 9.6/10

My parents, so sweetly, so trustingly and so very naively somehow let me have the majority of our year over for my 16th birthday. They were due to be out for the first half of the evening at one of Mum's gigs so would be back at around 11 and trusted me to look after the party until they were back. To be honest I was surprised anybody showed up, so to say that the whole thing was unexpected for the three of us is somewhat of an understatement. For most of the attendees (including me) it was our first real house party. How I managed to convince Mum and Dad to let me do it, I'll never know.

Some highlights:
- Roughly 60-80 15 and 16-year-old kids somehow fitting inside a relatively small three-bed detached house in a quiet suburban neighbourhood.

- My friend Nick swinging on the old tree in our back garden and ripping one of the huge branches off, the absolute bellend. Dad was furious.
- Jamie's room became the designated wine cellar; stocked to the brim with snuck-in Tesco carrier bags full of more cherry Lambrini than is ever socially acceptable.
- Loads of our picture frames around the house being smashed.
- Dad's barbecue getting broken.
- My mate Vicky vomiting down the side of my brother's bed and then having to be carried home.
- My mate Louis consequently passing out in Vicky's aforementioned sick on my brother's bed, before vomiting himself, rebounding back into action and then picking up a fresh bottle of WKD and carrying on like a trooper.
- Red and blue WKD being spilt everywhere (see previous point), leaving two huge red stains on our carpet which are still there to this day a decade later.
- Dancing in a manner that I can only assume was breathtakingly alluring and not at all awkwardly uncoordinated to Britney Spears - Piece of Me (as if it wasn't already obvious that this was the early 2000s).
- Making out with two different party guests that night (winner – I knew the sexy dancing would pay off).
- Nick (the tree guy) being carried, paralytic, into the back of his mum's car and being wrapped in a little blanket. Quite a difference from the smug shit he

was a few hours earlier and many of us enjoyed this immensely.
- Some of the guys from school turning up to the party very sweetly and generously with two enormous (and very heavy) pot plants as "gifts". It in fact turned out that they'd liberated the plants from one of our neighbours' houses on their way over, so of course the next day Mum had me and my friends go and wander around the estate with the dreaded things in an attempt to find the correct house to return the plants. What Mum doesn't know is that we searched for ages (around five minutes) round the whole estate but couldn't see any matching pot plants or obvious gaps where there once used to be pot plants. We had no idea where they came from and were bored by this point, so we left them in a random driveway and ran away.
- Some of the boys getting overexcited and betting eachother to do shots of Hennessey with added gourmet flavourings of mouthwash, ketchup and cat biscuits (?), in a bid to discover who would throw up first.
- One of my other friends, Iz, seeing a bottle of blue mouthwash at the top of the stairs (see previous point) which of course she assumed was WKD and proceeded to neck it. Disappointingly sober yet minty fresh, she proceeded to use her new-found cleanliness to get off with some of the party guests. I say 'some of' because none of us are 100% sure who, including her.
- Two of my friends who still had dental braces at this time having the football net collapse over them

whilst kissing and then other guests proceeding to kick footballs at them. One of the other guests later described this scene as "the most disgusting thing I've ever seen".

- Not long after the party began my peers quickly discovered that my parents had (for whatever reason) allowed me and my pals to doodle on my bedroom walls. Once they'd discovered this nugget of information it took around three and half minutes before my bedroom walls and ceiling were completely covered in vulgar, varied and crudely drawn penises; some green, some large, some small, some simple and some with extremely graphic detail. For the remainder of my teenage life living at home (until Jamie went to Uni and I got his bigger bedroom) my bedroom soon resembled what I imagine the inside of a 12-year-old boy's mind is like. I remember in particular there was one really large and really graphic one done on the sloped ceiling above my bed, so from then on, every night before I'd go to sleep I'd be staring into the eye (so to speak) of a large and hairy cartoon todger. How I turned out so well-adjusted I really don't know.
- Once they'd returned home later that evening, Mum would frequently come into the living room (designated dancefloor) and turn the music down which was being blasted from the stereo system at full deafening volume. Inevitably, one of the guests would immediately turn it right back up as soon as she left the room. This would happen multiple times

throughout the night until (almost) everyone was finally kicked out.
- Somehow managing to fit 30 kids sleeping over; with 20 crammed into sleeping bags on our living room floor and the rest in a mixture of little tents (they'd come prepared) or just in sleeping bags straight on the grass in the garden and my bedroom.
- Us not letting Mum and Dad sleep by being rowdy and excitable, so Mum would come downstairs, exhausted, to the living room where we were all still making as much noise as you'd expect 20 kids in this scenario to make. She'd turn the light on and shout at us that she'd only had two minutes of sleep, so we needed to please shut up and let her sleep. Once she'd gone upstairs this would be promptly followed by one of my mates turning the living room light on, sitting on a stool in the doorway, waving his hand like the queen and doing an impression of my Mum, shouting "I've only had two minutes of sleep!", which we would all find hilarious and this would wake Mum up again and then the whole cycle would repeat.
- The morning after, fresh and alert from our 37 minutes of sleep, my dad pulled me into the kitchen and stood at the kitchen window. He said, "Bex, come and look at this." One of my mates Joe was standing in the garden in his pants where he'd been for the last 10 minutes, despite it being November. He was hosing himself down with the garden hose, steam emanating from his pasty body, and whistling cheerfully. I don't know why either.

SO YOUR CHILD IS A COMPLETE ARSEHOLE

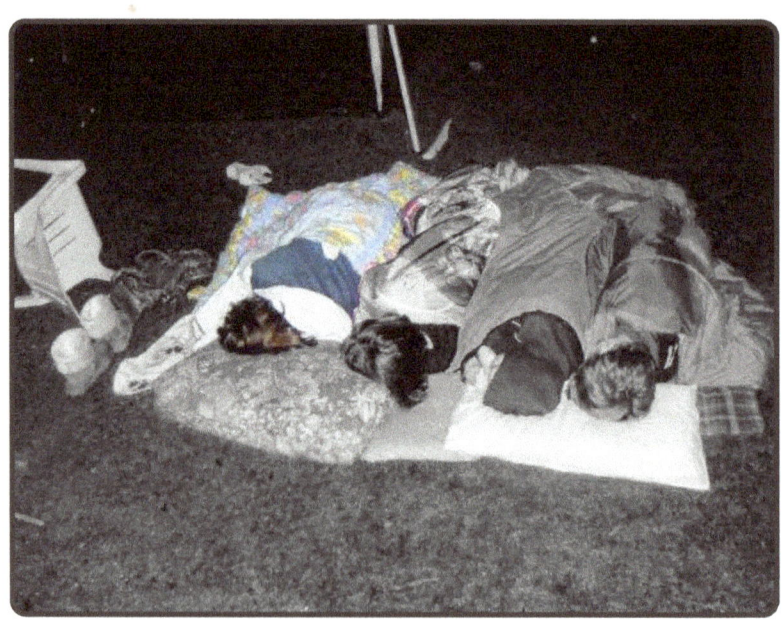

The time my cousin and I hotboxed a wendy house

TWATTERY SCORE: 4.20 / 10

When I was around 15, my cousin (we'll call him 'Josh' – because that's his name) and I used to hang out a fair amount, given we were the same age and in the same year at school. Thus, we found in each other kindred spirits and became close for a while; both of us would travel to each other's houses and hang out with each other's mates from time to time. In other words, he was also a little bit of a teenage arsehole. Sorry, Josh. In fact, I could tell you lots and lots of stories about Josh's antics. But I'm not going to so you'll have to just bloody well read his book, won't you.

On a family holiday where the whole extended family rented a huge holiday cottage in Devon, Josh and I snuck out in the middle of the night and found the only shelter we could find outside which ended up being a little kid's Wendy house. Here, we smoked a badly-rolled wonky joint (with, may I add, some rather delicious cranberry and vanilla flavoured tobacco). We also didn't realise that because the fake little plastic windows and door were so tiny and rubbish that we ended up hotboxing ourselves inside there and getting absolutely, ridiculously, mind-numbingly stoned. Thankfully I'm naturally always slow, tired and hungry (somewhat sloth-like by design) even when I'm completely sober so it's not much of a surprise that no-one noticed.

Hotboxing (n.)
The practice of smoking marijuana in an enclosed space
(e.g. a car or a small room) in order to maximise the narcotic effect.

BECCI ABBOTT

The time my teacher called me a part-timer

TWATTERY SCORE: 9.6/10

You may have picked up on this already, but dear lord was I lazy as a teenager. General disinterest, lethargy and constant boredom all mixed together and amounted in me pulling an absolutely idiotic number of sickies to get out of having to go to school. After years of trying to force me to go to school to which I would just shout into submission or completely ignore, Mum and Dad were at their wit's end, so by the time I got to 16 in Year 11 - GCSE year – my form tutor openly referred to me as the class 'part timer' whenever I decided to grace the class with my presence.

I was relying on being able to cram study before my exams and get passable grades and didn't know what I wanted to do so found it hard to focus.

This chapter is quite annoying to write in retrospect to be honest, because I learned that one doesn't get the same opportunity to learn so many cool things again once you leave school, not to mention that you're with all your mates and having a great social life. As boring and stressful as school can be, I really wish I'd have grabbed the opportunity to learn whilst I had it in my grasp, because I learned the hard way that motivating yourself to distance learn or self-study as an adult takes an incredible amount of motivation, which clearly I had a severe shortage of. People would tell me this all the time while I was there, but I didn't care; nothing was going to make me focus. I really wish I'd cared more about this and a lot of things.

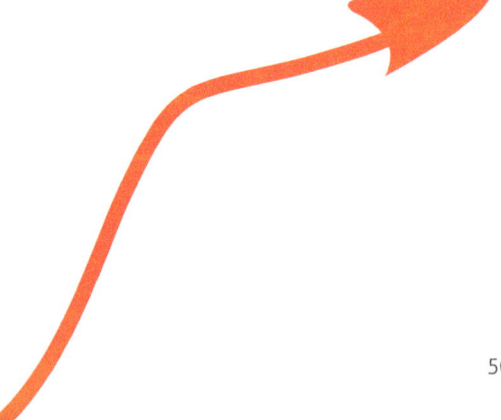

The times I didn't understand why Mum is so sensitive

TWATTERY SCORE: IDON'TGETIT/10

For me, although a short one, this point is probably one of the biggest and most important points in the entire book as it goes some way to explain an enormous amount of my behaviour.

I knew I could be difficult sometimes, but I also just didn't understand why Mum craved my affection and attention so much. Now that I'm a little older and we're extremely close it's obvious why she sought this relationship, but back at 17 I had other priorities aside from showing love to my Mum (yawn). I thought she just knew that by my being in the house still it meant I loved them and didn't know why she needed more, so just didn't understand. I thought I didn't have to keep saying it because obviously I love my parents, I didn't have a choice, they're my parents so I love them automatically. As far as I was concerned, if I didn't love them, they'd know about it, so I didn't need to show it any more than being present. Plus, it's easier to react to affection with an uncomfortable, dismissive shrug than it is to react with a big hug back and a genuine 'I love you' (eurgh, cringe).

But now as an ever-so-slightly-more-mature grown-up, something I now realise is that Mums (Dads as well of course but in my case, most definitely Mums) need to be told, and I really, really didn't understand that as a teenager. I just thought she knew.

The time we played 'lights'

TWATTERY SCORE: 8.7/10

'Lights', in case you don't know, Stan (which I'm sure you don't because you're not as much of a total moron as I was back then), is a game to be played with your pals during the night-time.

The rules of the game are complex but I'll try to break it down for you as best I can. You ready?
- Walk around your neighbourhood late at night (you with me so far?)
- Whenever a car comes, you're not allowed to let the beam of light hit you.

That's it. That's the whole game. The concept is simple but the execution, I must say, can be pretty magnificent.

The rules of the game require you to hide from the light at any cost, and I don't know if you've seen a car recently, but they move fast, and the beam of their headlights cover vast areas. Also, don't forget, you have to play at night so it is really, really dark, and a lot of the time you have no idea what your obstacles will be until you're already clambering into / over / underneath it. Thus, we had players knock random fences down (albeit accidentally) in their panic to get away from the light, or roll under parked cars, throw themselves into hedges, catapult up trees, parkour across garden furniture to get behind shelter, dive headfirst into gardens etc.

My cousin Josh joined us on one particular occasion, the highlight of this night being that my mate Iz, whilst sprinting away from an approaching car, pelted headfirst into a tree in the pitch dark and straight into a protruding horizontal twig that went straight into her eyeball and made us all really, really laugh.

BONUS STORY: The time Dad thought it would be funny to newspaper over my doorway while I was asleep

HE GETS HIS OWN TWATTERY SCORE: A RESPECTABLE 8.6/10

SO YOUR CHILD IS A COMPLETE ARSEHOLE

The time I made that bad decision

TWATTERY SCORE: 9.9/10

I was five weeks into sixth form. I left for lunch one day and met up with my mates; none of whom were in school nor worked.

I was always so jealous that they had nowhere to go and I hated the thought of turning around and going back to the afternoon's lessons. I'd been mainly interested in studying English and had dreams of becoming a journalist, but when our incredible long-standing and much beloved English teacher left after we finished our GCSEs and the new, rubbish English teacher (she really was rubbish to be fair, she got fired a few months after this particular lunch break) replaced her, my one final teeny tiny spark of interest in my education flickered out and disappeared.

So, this one lunch break in late summer, rather than turning around and going back to school, I kept walking. I kept walking with my friends in the complete opposite direction of the school and I never walked back through the school gates again.

SO YOUR CHILD IS A COMPLETE ARSEHOLE

The times we were disturbed by our neighbour

TWATTERY SCORE: 8.8/10

Do you by any chance have a friend that has a really, really, really loud cackling laugh that bounces off every wall and sounds like a deafening cacophony of aural abuse? Well that's me and my friend Iz. We're that friend. Worse than this also, we have the exact same booming laugh except that my laugh deepens towards the end whereas Iz's goes higher, which naturally we find absolutely hilarious, so when both of us start laughing at the same time (usually about nothing) often what happens is that our laughs being the exact same tone and resonance makes us laugh all the more, so our laughs end up ricocheting off each other in some weird twisted harmony and gradually worsen and worsen as we get more hysterical at the ridiculousness and the loudness. The tension and the excitement mounts as our collective witches' cackle grows into a frenzied torrent of quickening booms and hysterical crying, the noise of it all bouncing from wall to wall and echoing through whichever estate we're in at the time (usually Mum and Dad's back then) in a volume that would make the personified sound of nails on a chalkboard cover its metaphorical ears and howl in agony.

So, when our next door neighbour leans his groggy head out of their upstairs bedroom window at my friends and I (who are sat around the garden table in Mum and Dad's back garden) and screams, 'OI!!! BECCI!!!! It's 3 in the fucking morning, SHUT UP!!!!', imagine our shock and surprise at our lovely quiet evening being ruined by our noisy neighbour yelling at us. Honestly, some people.

Iz being the ginger cherry on top of our little human pile and no I couldn't breathe, Stan, thanks for asking.

The 'S' word

TWATTERY SCORE: 69/10

Sorry gang, I think I've gotta talk about sex for a moment. Yup, sex. The big S. The rumpy pumpy. Canoodling. The ol' razzle dazzle.

Mum, Dad and other family members, you might want to skip this chapter. We will meet you guys at the Underpass which is coming up next. See you there!

20 seconds later

Right, I've just checked and don't worry – they're all gone. It's just you and me now, Stan.

As much as I'd love to avoid this chapter I do think discussing the dreaded 'S' is an important point to make when talking about my teen years as it really did steer the ship most of the time, even if not directly. Of course, you do a lot of fumbling experimental "stuff" in your early teen years, but we're talking about the big dog here.

The first thing to say is that I had really, really, really low self-confidence. I mean, who doesn't? You've probably already gathered anyway from this book that I was a steaming pile of self-hating, mirror-smashing, face-punching despair during this period of my life.

So, when I threw sex into the mix, it doesn't go that well. Not terribly, but not great.

It took years and years and years before I could even start to actually *enjoy* sex. For a long time, I was way too aware of what I was doing and someone looking at my horrible body in its entirety. I was always so distracted and nervous and never, ever in the moment. Also, in those first instances we're kids – we don't know what the shit is going on.

One big point to make which is slightly verging on taboo but important to say: I honestly felt like I'd been lied to after having sex the first few times. Lied to by everyone. TV, Media and popular culture up until that point showed sex as being fully enjoyable for both parties every time; the couple always reaching an agreed and perfectly timed climax and then shaking hands, sharing a cigarette and reading the Guardian. Man alive did I feel lied to when *it* finally happened and it was *not* like that. I know that some of my close heterosexual female mates felt the same as well; we felt like society had lied to us our entire lives. Most movies (as far as we were concerned) showed straight women enjoying the whole sexual process immediately and gave us the expectation that sex would feel immediately incredible and be like pressing a button to make you happy, when actually, when it finally actually happened to us, it actually seemed to turn out that sex wasn't for us to enjoy; it was for our partner to enjoy. My partners, all male in my case, were the ones that got the enjoyment. For us it was just sore and awkward and invasive and weird. Again, this is talking purely from a heterosexual standpoint and in my personal experience. It seems to me to be getting a little better on popular culture nowadays in being a more honest reflection on what the first times are like for straight women (I wouldn't be able to comment on the experiences of other genders and sexualities), but it's still not really addressed that for a really long time and for a lot of us, sex really doesn't feel that great at first. It was quite a disappointment being hit with the stark reality that first time. And no-one said this to each-other, so it was really hard to process and left me with a weird lack of self-importance once I realised that no-one really cares about my feelings and I wasn't necessarily meant to enjoy it. There was a huge amount of guilt and shame interspersed with these feelings also that I wrestled with for a long time. It's difficult to enjoy something when you feel ashamed of it.

All of the above is precisely why I always made it my mission from then on to make sure I spoke to my younger female cousins – who are like sisters to me – openly and honestly about this kind of stuff, because for me, not having that perspective and understanding genuinely knocked my already low confidence even lower and gave me a really confusing relationship with sex for a long time. Don't get me wrong, the experiences weren't horrible; just not what I expected. I did enjoy the excitement of having someone you fancy showing affection in that way, but that's all it ever was really. Just a step up from kissing.

Also, don't forget that when you're a teenager exploring all this stuff, YOU. BOTH. LIVE. AT. HOME. Eeeeeeew. Parents and siblings might be around and there's always the disgraceful possibility of someone walking in or seeing you or just, eurgh *shudders*. It's no wonder I hated people barging into my room unannounced or being reminded that you live with your parents, I always just wanted to be left alone so that I could work my shit out or flirt online undisturbed. Back then if we weren't doing sex then we were probably talking about it, or thinking about it, or planning to go out in case you get it.

Maybe you're thinking, 'erm, sorry, Becci, absolutely not; my first time was beautiful and there were fireworks & rainbows and we skipped through a meadow afterwards and it was full of Romeo & Juliet passion, you were just shit in bed'. And I'm sure that's probably the case but either way, this was my feeling about it for a long time.

This feeling also aided in setting my bar for relationships quite low, as I'd discovered (or so I thought) that I wasn't the most important one in the bedroom, which is fine, so I'm obviously not the most important one in the relationship, which is also fine. I was just grateful to get any attention. I had come to the understanding now that romantic, true love isn't real and that, also, is fine, I'll settle with the best I can. This naturally led to all sorts of rubbish relationships and romances which went nowhere and usually ended in me being hurt, upset and embarrassed. I felt this way for years; just pure gratitude for anyone who showed me affection and no confidence to even begin to think about what *I* wanted. If I didn't expect to be treated nicely and respected (e.g. have my messages responded to or shown any affection and kindness whatsoever) then why would my boyfriend at the time? They didn't have to, so they didn't.

Obviously I'm very relieved to say that eventually, once I was truly confident and happy with myself and started to date mature people who respected me entirely, everything changed and something switched where I realised what it was all about and started to realise, 'oh! This is nice…'. So things definitely got better; I think it's often part of the process that we have to go through shit relationships and slowly raise the bar each time until you realise how you should be treated / treat each other and also what a healthy relationship is. Unless you're one of the lucky ones and find the good one early on. I did have some lovely, great relationships with very sweet people before my now-fiancé (including my first ever husband-boyfriend 'S' of 'Shrek 3' fame) but Connaire completely changed the game. He loves me irrefutably and for the first time in a relationship I have complete faith in that. I am now, finally, indescribably happy and so very loved.

It took me a while, but I found him eventually.

Vomit.

The time we went to the underpass

TWATTERY SCORE: 8.5/10

Welcome back, family! Lovely to see you again. Don't worry, you didn't miss anything exciting.

Right, so, where were we?

Ohhhh yes of course; I know exactly where we are. We're standing in the empty, cold, dark, grey, concrete of the underpass. Basically just a 20-metre-wide concrete tunnel with a flat, low ceiling and more visible graffiti than concrete. There's daylight either side where the world exists but it's dark in the centre. There's a thin, overgrown and very muddy path leading in both directions out of the underpass, the area surrounded by trees and fields and more trees. There's a ridiculous number of decaying Marlboro Light cigarette butts and plastic Tesco carrier bags everywhere and so very many abandoned empty Budweiser bottles strewn over both the dusty floor of the underpass and in the woodlands either side. And it's loud – really loud – the M25 is running above us so the constant, deafening roar of cars echo in the walls. I remember we'd play music off our phones (before portable speakers were a thing) but you could never hear it over the motorway.

Don't worry, I know what you're thinking, right and you're right.

This place is fucking heaven.

A magical, private place full of fun, teenage adventure, privacy and privacy and also just SO. MUCH. PRIVACY.

We used to go to the underpass a loooot. I think it's quite common for kids to have an inherent desire to constantly seek out a spot that can be used as a sort of 'clubhouse' and the search for said clubhouse tends to be the general unofficial aim when wandering about outside (this is probably because our parents don't want us to hang out at their houses with them just yet). This natural desire in our case led us to hang around in all sorts of spaces – the tiny patch of grass outside Costcutters; Iver station; this little bit of woodland round the corner from Iver church; the sports club, etc.

For a good while on the days when our clubhouse of the moment wasn't Vicky's Mum's house (Julie went on holiday with her mates a fair amount so Vicky would have awesome house parties whenever she went away) we settled on The Underpass. It was convenient for us as it was a 30-minute walk from Mum and Dad's in Richings Park (the area where most of us lived and the rest frequented, giving our group the nickname 'The Richings Lot' which the OGs of us who remain still refer to each other as to this day). It was so very private and very quiet; the perfect place for us to hang out undisturbed and away from the eyes of disapproving parents. There we would smoke and drink and listen to music and generally just hang out together. It also had the hint of danger, as given the length of time it took to get to in a very uninhabited area, it would be really quite a brilliant place to murder someone (you're welcome, murderers), which is often why it was so very private – particularly at night. It's probably most parents' nightmare, which of course only made it more appealing. Parents' nightmares are naturally usually the places that teenagers frequent, in both senses of the phrase. Danger and risk drew us like moths to a flame as it seems to do when you're young. Don't forget that you're invincible back then and the crushing weight of your own mortality (aka adulthood) hasn't quite started to strangle your soul yet.

In addition to this, part of the beauty of being a teenager was that none of your peers had jobs or responsibilities, so everyone's time outside of school was guaranteed free time. When you're 15, people don't say all their usual boring excuses you get as adults, such as: "oh I can't come out today because the husband and I are taking the kids to Fred's barbecue" or "I've got a busy day at work on Monday so it's a no from me I'm afraid" and "I don't like you, Becci, please stop calling me". When you're 15, whenever you're asked if you want to come and have fun you answer, every time, "fuck yeah". You've no excuse not to come out and play, so you do. A lot. For this reason, there were always big groups of random people from different parts of our lives; my school friends mixed with my local Richings Park friends mixed with *their* school friends and then *their* friends from home etc. etc. Just loads of kids whose entire purpose at that point was to have fun. We all said, "fuck yeah", every time.

On one particular occasion, before we knew our limits and back when drinking was a sport, a group of us went to the underpass. My friend Mike had no idea what a normal amount of alcohol for one person is, so asked his brother to buy him a 12-crate of a beer and a bottle of vodka all for himself (which I'm sure you'll agree seems perfectly reasonable and not at all an outrageous amount for a 16 year old with very little drinking experience).

Of course, he ended up vomiting profusely and falling unconscious, so guess who got a panicked, emergency call at 2am asking them to come to the Underpass, call an ambulance and follow the ambulance containing Mike to the hospital? Mummy Abbott, that's who. Funny how we only remembered that Mum existed during these moments. She followed the ambulance with two of my other friends half-conscious in the back of her car, their empty wine and vodka bottles clinking in their bags. She also had to deal with Mike's dad shouting at her when she stopped by his house to let him know about his son. I know what you're thinking, Stan, my poor bloody mum.

Where was I, I hear you ask? Well I'd originally come home a little earlier in the evening with my two aforementioned drunk friends. They'd fallen asleep on the sofa and so, bored, I went back out to hang with my mates at the Underpass again, leaving Mum, my friends and those who'd been with Mike to deal with the mess. Noice.

SO YOUR CHILD IS A COMPLETE ARSEHOLE

The time we snuck onto the sports field

TWATTERY SCORE: 7.9/10

One time my friends and I snuck onto the local community sports field late at night, which we used to do a lot, actually. We loved hanging out on the field as we could drink, smoke and play music late into the night. Take it from me; we fucking loved us a field.

The only problem was that the local community didn't like us being on the field as much as we did. There was one particular night when we were innocently hanging out on the sports field (by 'innocently hanging out' I of course mean 'sat up on top of the huge cricket team storage units where we had snuck up onto and were drinking, smoking and taking it in turns setting fire to the lace tennis court safety netting') and we suddenly heard shouting and the bright lights of torches shining in our faces.

What would you do in this situation, Stan? If you were a teenager hanging with your mates somewhere you shouldn't, and you were inevitably caught out? Well it's funny you should stay that, Stan, because that is precisely what we did: we panicked and scattered. Running as fast as we could and laughing so much we could barely breathe, we catapulted ourselves over the closest fences and walls into random neighbouring gardens that backed onto the field; dive bombing over hedges, accidentally battering each other with our elbows in the frenzy and hiding under cars, in bushes and behind trees. Thankfully 'Lights' was excellent training for this kind of sudden escape.

Somehow we weren't caught, us cheeky sods, but we ended up with several cuts and bruises each as our trophies – including one of us (me) sporting a lovely black shiner above my eye from where Lewis bashed into me in all his lanky excitement.

SO YOUR CHILD IS A COMPLETE ARSEHOLE

The house on Wellesley Avenue

TWATTERY SCORE: OUCH/10

My incredibly beautiful best mate & one true love, my Vicks, used to have brilliant house parties when we were teenagers in her childhood home on Wellesley Avenue. Her house was around the corner from mine so each other's houses were just an extension of our own. We would casually wander between both houses all the time; sometimes multiple times a day, and whenever Vicks would have house parties a crowd of people would stay in her house and the remainder would come staggering back to mine and collapse on all the spare beds, sofas and floors we could find. Mum and Dad got very used to waking up in the house and wandering downstairs to find a bunch of sleeping teenage strangers who'd appeared during the night.

As I've mentioned in the Underpass chapter, Vicky's Mum Julie used to go on holiday with her friends quite a lot, so whenever she did their house would become party central. So many incredibly fun house parties and gatherings were had at Vicky's. This truly is one of the most nostalgic elements of our teenagerhood as we would sit around that kitchen table with the multicoloured-polka-dot-patterned tablecloth, smoke (Julie smoked so she wouldn't notice – what a bloody treat smoking inside was), drink and laugh. So many wonderful memories were made there with so many people who were some of our closest mates at the time but who are just blurred memories to us now.

One evening when Julie was away and Vicky was having one of her house parties, Vicks and some schoolmates were out in the garden on the trampoline when we heard some God-awful screaming. It turned out that Vicky had drunkenly jumped barefoot off of the trampoline in the pitch black and straight onto the shattered bottom half of a glass bottle, piercing her foot in the process and ending up with pretty disgustingly deep cuts.

Once again, guess who got a terrified call at 3am, dragged themselves out of bed, drove to Julie's house to take Vicky to the hospital where we then ended up being held until 2pm the following day, having had only a couple of hours' sleep? Mummy Abbott, that's who. Think you're starting to understand the pattern here, aren't you?

SO YOUR CHILD IS A COMPLETE ARSEHOLE

The time I was a layabout

TWATTERY SCORE: 9.5/10

Some people contribute to society by forging a career in the emergency services or NHS. Some people go into politics in order to make change, or work for charities, or are activists, or are deeply involved in their local community.

My contribution to society between August 2010 and January 2011 amounted to sitting in my then-boyfriend's mum's empty house (when I say empty I mean empty; she'd had tenants renting the place who had ripped all of the furnishings and electrics out so the only thing left was a sofa, a TV and an Xbox), smoking weed with my boyfriend and his mates and playing Nazi Zombies. I'm sure you've read about me and all my charitable efforts in the papers. I wish I could articulate how many times we played and how good we got at World at War & Black Ops Nazi Zombies. We played them so many freaking times, all the while listening to Eminem - Recovery and Sean Kingston's self-titled album on repeat so. many. times., that even recalling this period of my life gets tracks from those albums stuck in my head. How very, very, very repetitive it was.

My boyfriend at the time, we'll call him J, had lived with his dad a little while away from his hometown of Colnbrook, but the relationship with J and his dad's new wife was strained to say the least. J had been about to leave his dad's house to join the army and was just visiting his mum who lived in Colnbrook when we met. He then, having met my ravishing self, decided not to join the army and stay with his mum so that we could be together (who can blame him). She lived with her boyfriend and her house remained empty, so that's where we would stay for days or weeks on end.

This was, as you'd expect, a tumultuous period full of friction between my parents and I, especially given I needed money to eat / buy cigs and expected to contribute nothing in return. J and I would do the long walk through some horse fields between Colnbrook and Iver from his mum's house to my parents' house, ask for money for food, grab packets of crisps and maybe my Playstation and then head back through the fields to his mum's where we'd stay for the next week, sporadically having friends over and never, ever studying or working. Mum would constantly text me and call me and ask me to please come home as she was worried about me, but I would just ignore it or tell her I'm fine, leave me alone. I didn't get why she didn't just get on with life and let me get on with mine.

This cycle went on for months. I started to go down the road of accepting that this was all I was meant for and what my life would always be; probably on benefits (out of laziness rather than inability to work), smoking weed with J and his mates, probably getting pregnant and having babies because that's what people do and just eventually withering away somewhere. I couldn't be bothered to think of doing anything else and my soul and brain slowed to a standstill.

My parents saw that if I continued doing what I was doing, one of two 16-year-olds basically living on their own in an empty house, they'd lose me forever. They wanted the best for me but could see me wasting my life away in a confused haze.

My parents saw this chain of events unfolding before them and made a very, very, very wise and kind decision. They asked J to move in with us.

BECCI ABBOTT

The time we had a bonfire in the garden

TWATTERY SCORE: 8.6/10

We used to have bonfires at the back of Mum and Dad's garden pretty regularly. I'm pretty sure there's still a mushroom-shaped hole in the trees in our back garden from where we threw deodorant cans into the flames as teenagers just love to do (I don't know what to tell you, we just really bloody love it) and the inevitable explosion made a great big booming fireball into the trees which, much to Dad's fury, has never grown back.

I also personally always loved a good dramatic staring-into-the-bonfire profile picture during my emo days, so it served multiple purposes.

BONUS STORY: The time I was extremely confused

TWATTERY SCORE: ¿/10

Picture this for a moment, Stan.

You're 16. You wake up one Saturday in the summer, hungry and sleepy. You were out late at the Underpass last night so it's not until midday that you finally drag yourself out of bed; groggy and a little dazed. You think you're going to Slough Cinema with your mates later that day so you go to brush your teeth, thinking about what movies are going to be out and how you're going to ask Mum and Dad for the money. This is when you hear a really weird noise that you don't recognise coming from downstairs. You walk down the stairs, getting increasingly more confused as the noise gets even louder, rubbing your eyes and yawning.

You open the kitchen door, blink for a moment to see if you're still dreaming but nope – you're not dreaming. The noise is SO fast and SO loud. There's a complete stranger sat on a kitchen chair in the centre of the empty kitchen on his own playing Spanish music on an accordion.

You blink and stare, startled, frozen in the doorway and slightly threatened by this accordion-wieldin nutter who's on your land first thing in the morning (well, ish).

If the accordion-wielding-nutter was even the slightest bit fazed by you and looked up he would have seen a small, beige, wide-eyed child with her hair sticking up at perpendicular angles (probably with a few twigs nestled inside the mangey barnet) standing stock-still in her Harry Potter pyjamas, frozen in the kitchen doorway still in a half-walking position.

After many minutes of startled bewilderment I managed to un-freeze myself and searched around the house to find Mum and Dad had been there all along – they'd been in the office which is next to the kitchen but not visible from the doorway which is why I'd not seen them at first. Turns out Mum had found this poor fella in some random place somewhere, discovered he's a musician and invited him over to the house to play music, as she'd done so many times before (this is a thing she does). She just yet again neglected to tell me and caught me somewhat off-guard...or she'd told me and I'd ignored her – that happened too.

SO YOUR CHILD IS A COMPLETE ARSEHOLE

The time we saw that Evening Standard article

TWATTERY SCORE: 0/10

Everything changed when I moved back home. Back in a normal home environment and bored with our entire lives' purpose having been nothing except scrounging for the next meal, Mum and Dad encouraged J to find work (he was actually a brilliant mechanic and car enthusiast so he managed to find an apprenticeship with a mechanic not too far from us).

As for me, one day Dad came home all excitable, clutching that day's edition of the Evening Standard. In the back of this particular Evening Standard was a full-page advertisement for a brand new A&R / Music Business apprenticeship that was being held in a recording studio in London in conjunction with a major label. This was of great interest to us both because as you will undoubtedly remember from bullet point 12 of 'The Emo Stage', I was very into music. Joking aside, I really was.

I come from a very, very musical family full of a lot of irritatingly talented musicians (genes of which unfortunately decided to skip me entirely). Both Mum and Jamie are professional musicians now; Jamie working as a freelance musician in Abu Dhabi and Mum as a freelance composer / music teacher. My gran on my dad's side is an absolutely incredible singer and was very active in choirs throughout her life. Her son, my uncle, is also a talented professional musician out in South Africa, where he bore two also very annoyingly talented musicians; my cousins, Jade and Rox. Rox is a professional musician down in Brighton with her boyfriend, also a professional musician. My nana (Mum's mum) was a piano teacher. My uncles, aunts and cousins are all incredibly talented musicians and / or beautiful singers, so big family & friend jams on our holidays and family gatherings are commonplace.

This incredible virtuoistic talent was woven throughout my mum and her 4 siblings and then also their offspring; a glorious, beautiful web of music which is a core string that connects all members of our family and friends.

Anyway, I'm sure you get the point that music was in my bones (or maybe constantly very close to my bones); I just couldn't play it very well. The idea of an apprenticeship in an actual commercial recording studio and to be in the music industry behind the scenes was like a dream come true. The kind of environment I obviously wanted to be a part of (who didn't) but I didn't believe that there was any way it could have actually happened.

But there it was; shining out of the Evening Standard in huge beautiful black letters. 'A&R Apprenticeship in Music Business; no experience necessary'. So, along with around 200 other applicants, I applied.

I somehow managed to blag an interview for this apprenticeship (Mum had to come with me because I was 16) and, down purely to the fact that my mum was so brilliant and got on so well with one of the interviewers I was one of 10 applicants who got a place.

Game changer.

I didn't deserve this opportunity. After stupidly dropping out of school with no plans, no A-Levels and no job (which I would never, ever recommend to anyone else thinking of doing the same; it was really bloody stupid) and sitting on my arse for months, the fact that I managed to swan into an incredible opportunity that would pave a decade-long (and still going) career in and around the music industry was jammy to say the least. I actually met my now-fiancé Connaire whilst I was working at Strongroom Studio in East London and he was there recording with his band (thank you to the incredible Steph for setting us up on a blind-ish date. It went ok).

Of course, I did actually work really, really, really hard as soon as I got my start, but it was pure luck and the love of my parents that got me that first step. Quickly after having something to focus on that I was passionate about, the blurred edges started to sharpen and the less-twatty adult I was meant to become started to be formed.

I mean, less twatty, but not completely free of twattitude.

SO YOUR CHILD IS A COMPLETE ARSEHOLE

The time I got a tattoo

> **TWATTERY SCORE:**
> **WELLTOBEHONESTITSAMATTEROFPERSON‑**
> **ALPREFERENCESOMEPEOPLEHATETHEMSOM‑**
> **EDON'TALLOPINIONSAREVALID/10**

My dad hates tattoos. He really hates them; hates them with every fibre in his body. He often told me that if I ever "got a tattoo" he'd "chuck me out the house". So, naturally, it will come as no surprise to you, Stan, that I got tattoos. I got plenty (and counting).

The first tattoo I got (7 black birds across my back, shoulder-to-shoulder, because I am exceptionally original and unique) was when I was 17-ish, after I'd broken up with J (a long-time coming as we were friends more than we were in a relationship). I was bored and desperately wanting to exert my independence having been strapped into a not-that-great relationship for so long, so, on a whim one night when I was hanging out with a friend who had a car, I asked if he'd take me to this guy I'd heard about in Langley who would give tattoos from his house to people under 18 if you brought him a box of beer. If that in itself isn't enough accreditation for you, he was also an ex-hells-angel with no teeth.

He did shots of Jagermeister whilst he did the tattoo because it "steadied his hand". At one point, knowing I was lying on my front and thus couldn't see what he was doing, he said, cigarette balanced precariously out of his mouth (I imagine... I couldn't see him), "Jesus Christ, this is the best giraffe I've ever done", giggling to himself when I shat myself. Don't worry, Stan, there was of course no giraffe. In the end I think it turned out rather nicely, all things considered. I've since added a watercolour background to my 7 black birds.

To be fair to my ex-hells-angel-turned-tattoo-artist, I do enjoy painting this picture but he was actually a) lovely, b) a brilliant artist with gorgeous pencil drawings sketched over his entire living room wall and c) wouldn't actually give tattoos to anyone well underage despite the rumours, but as I was just a few months away from 18 he yielded.

And yes, my Dad absolutely LOVES my tattoos. He just loves them. He often says to me, "Crikey, Becci, I was anti-tattoo before, but your general airs of poise and dignity really pull off tattoos in a graceful way that I never thought possible. I am a changed man and you are a revelation, thank you for showing me the error of my ways," and I go, "Dad, please, it's my honour and privilege to inform and open the eyes of the ignorant – nono, get up off your knee, there's no need to grovel but merely revel in your newfound understanding" and he says, "thank you

Becci, your wisdom and kindness know no bounds. I am humbly indebted to you" and I go "alright, Dad, cut it out".

JK, he still really hates them.

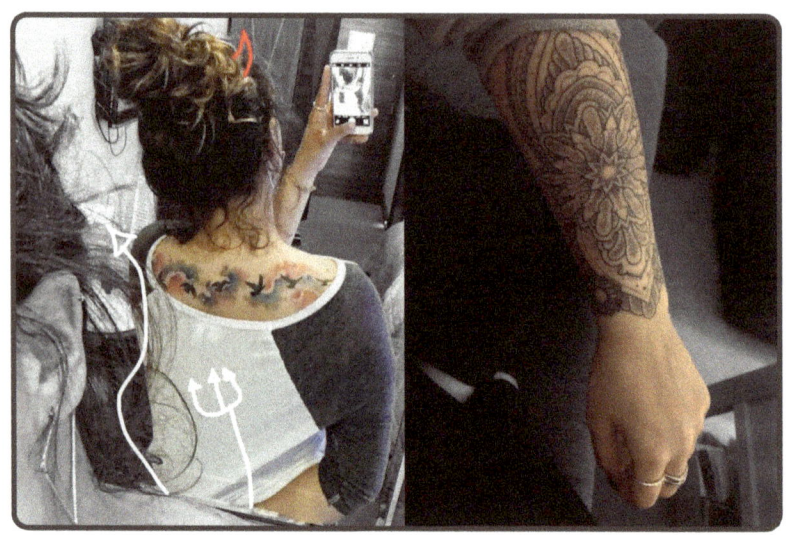

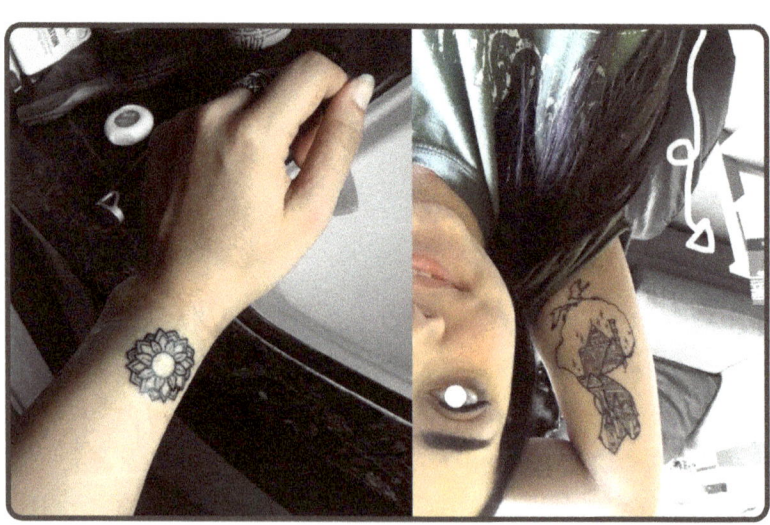

BECCI ABBOTT

The time it got better

TWATTERY SCORE: -10/10

As our journey comes to a close, my dearest Stan, I thought it might be good just to wrap up a few pointers and outline why things got a bit better between myself and my parents. Every parent/child relationship is different, completely unique and extremely nuanced so it's hard to say strictly what changed and whether the same would be said for other families, but there are certainly some factors in our case that must've helped ease the tension.

- The apprenticeship. Having purpose, focus and doing something that I genuinely loved changed so much. I had a reason for getting up in the morning; and not just because I knew I should.
- My incredibly patient family, both immediate and extended. They're really, really quite wonderful.
- Julie, who pushed me to be better.
- I can't really write this book without at least mentioning my mates. Mike, Louis, Luke, Iz, Vicky and Shawnee – the Richings Lot (I see you rolling your eyes, Stan, but yes we still go by that name just get off

our back). My mates are brilliant, smart and very, very funny people. Having such great influences around me with strong work ethics and high expectations forced me to grow up. I had no choice. Luke actually was my main Editor for this very book you're holding and was hugely involved in this whole process right from back when it was just a title I'd thought of and he replied to my text with, and I quote: "I fucking love that", so thank you, Luke for your endless support. They're truly my favourite people on the planet. My partners in crime, my kindred spirits, my childhood crew.

- Following on from the previous point, another huge factor that played into my improved relationship with Mum and Dad is how close my mates are with my family. This mostly comes down to us all being a bunch of dorks with a shared love of card/board games, food and music but my friends (particularly Vicky, Mike, Louis and Luke) are considered part of our family by my parents, aunts, uncles and cousins. So much so that Mike, Louis and Vicky come on our annual family holiday with us and have done for years. I know I am lucky to have this crossover between my mates and my whole family and it's something I'm really thankful for. I'm grateful that my family are all so brilliant and welcoming, and my mates are generally just so fucking great. It also really helped things with Mum and Dad because a) we would all spend all our time at home so Mum and Dad always knew where we were, b) my friends are pretty good influences and are all hard workers so my parents didn't have to worry and c) it was a great way of me spending more time with Mum and Dad; particularly Dad as a bunch of us would just play cards and games with Dad most weekends. This was the case for many years. This of course goes both ways as I also have a huge love and respect for all of their families and every single one welcomes the rest of us into their lives, homes and fridges.

- Moving out helped, obviously. It meant that seeing Mum and Dad was always a choice.
- Age.
- I finally became happy.

FIN.

The male parental unit

TWATTERY SCORE: "MARGDOYOURBLOODYPREDICTIONS"/10

Ah, Dad. My lovely Dad. There he is, in his happy place (the west country somewhere) looking over his shoulder and more than likely shouting at Mum for doing something. There's a lot to say about my dad. To make it easier for you to digest, Stan, I'll list him in Top Trumps form.

Job Title

- Uhh....Computing Architectural...Programming Smart, erm, Technology....er. I don't bloody know.

Traits

- Intelligent. Very intelligent. Very very intelligent.
- Quiet (or so he'd lead you to believe).
- Brilliant chef. Louis makes the journey over to Mum and Dad's to have his famous Salmon dinner whenever Dad makes it, whether I'm there or not.
- Funny.
- Generous. Dad has always cooked huge batches of dinner and welcomed anyone and everyone to join us. My friends, Jamie's friends, Mum's friends, you name it. Our house was and is an open-door-house and despite it being a total shithole people still seem to flock there. Mostly for Dad's food.
- Fun. So much fun. He, myself and Mike – who is annoyingly equally intelligent – all plan and host the huge quiz every year during our annual family holiday.
- Stubborn.
- Reliable.
- Confident. He's the antithesis of my mum who doubts every single thing she does, but Dad grounds her and tells her definitively that everything is ok. When Dad says everything is ok then it is. That's that. Dad has

no idea how much we need this and how floundering we'd be without him.
- Supportive. Dad's knees aren't great, but he will be at every single gig Mum does, and he'll film each one and show it to anyone and everyone who comes to the house, beaming with pride. He was once showing me a video he took at one of Mum's tiny gigs at a local summer festival. He said to me, "sorry the camera goes a bit shaky here because I had to stand holding the camera above my head for hours because there was nowhere for me to put the tripod at the back". He can't stand for long periods of time so this would have been agony for him, but he did it anyway – no question. Sob.
- A grumpy old git.
- He would never openly admit it but he really loves his family. He really really loves his family (this includes Connaire, Mike, Louis, Vicks and Luke).
- Ever-so-slightly* competitive.

*extremely fucking very

Hobbies

- Photography
- Genealogy
- Shouting at Mum that she needs to enter her bloody predictions in the football score prediction league thing he runs (she is ALWAYS late).
- Writing 'Well Done' in green highlighter across the entire page of every single birthday / congratulations

/ new baby / new house / sympathy card we ever send as a family (he's done this without fail for genuinely years).
- Playing board / card / virtual / any games with me, Connaire, Mike, Louis, Jim and Mum.
- Sitting still for long periods with the occasional nap thrown in.

Likes

- Man U / football in general.
- Tennis.
- Badminton.
- Athletics.
- Other such sport-like sports I couldn't give a whoopsie about.
- Blackadder.
- Monty Python.
- Planning quizzes with his daughter and Mike.
- Devon.
- Music and playing music loud. Particularly...
- Early Peter-Gabriel-era Genesis. I can't really articulate how special my relationship with Genesis's music is as a result of Dad having sat me down and listened through all their stuff with me over the years. Don't get me wrong; I first found them super boring when I was younger but as soon as I saw their tribute band 'The Musical Box' live and really heard it and saw the theatrics of it my eyes lit up and that was it – I was

done. Considering he's not the musician in the family he has a deep connection with music and part of the reason I love Genesis so much is based purely on how much he loves them and how passionately he cares. I've never met anybody that analyses music in the same way my dad does, or as well. Mum and Jamie do too from a replication standpoint, but Dad just has a way about him when he listens to something he loves. I've seen The Musical Box several times now and just recently took Connaire to his first ever show up here at Kings Theatre in Glasgow. It's a very special thing and a part of our relationship now that I treasure.
- Rare 12oz rump or T-bone steak (like father like daughter).
- Twiglets.
- Mint aero (Vicks buys him one as a gift every time she visits).
- Reviewing things as "bollocks" even when he's never heard of them before.
- The cats, even the horrible one.
- His best friend Ali.

Dislikes

- Books ("load of bollocks")
- Movies except the ones he likes ("It's bollocks.").
- TV shows except the ones he likes ("they're bollocks").
- Healthy food.
- Small portions.

- Rap.
- Most things.
- Me and my friends singing with each other when we're on Skype playing board games (he gets very cross).
- When games or quizzes are unfair or too "silly".

Special skills

- Farting at opportune moments (when you're about to say something he doesn't like / after someone's given devastating news and the moment is tensely serious / when he's frightened or surprised / all the fucking time).
- Planning the annual family holiday. They'd never happen if left to any of the rest of us.
- Planning and structuring quizzes. He's quite phenomenal.
- Researching and buying the best guitars (for Mum), laptops, microphones (for Mum), computer programs, recording equipment (for Mum) and all sorts of gadgets and various technology. He does a lot of stuff for Mum.
- Pie.

Dad and I used to argue A LOT when I was a teenager and I know that Dad used to find it difficult to know what to say to me or how to handle me. Dad is definitely a firmer hand than Mum is, but I was a screamer, a runner-away-er, a rule defy-er and an all-out knob. It really didn't matter what you as a parent would try to do to punish me because I would just steal my straighteners back, or go out anyway, or steal money they wouldn't give me or find other ways of getting / doing what I wanted. It was a very difficult time and everyone in the house was stressed, angry and miserable for probably a good few years.

Nowadays, my dad is my bud. My team mate. We're close – a little duo who understand each other (but also understand how to brilliantly annoy each other as a result) and work really well together. We're both stubborn and competitive and love food (a little too much). We are both quite confident with the stuff we say and are perfectly happy to shout if we feel like shouting. Dad can be difficult to get but I get him. Dad gave me the small part of my brain that's pretty good with computers and can analyse large amounts of data (when I have to) and so he's the main reason I'm able to do any of the jobs I've done to any degree of success. We enjoy planning, organising and coming up with creative solutions or puzzles.

For someone who claims he's not romantic or affectionate, and for someone who probably shouts at Mum more than he talks to her, Dad's unwavering love for my mum is like really quite something. He's at every gig she ever plays, he makes huge vats of food for her and her band whenever they have practices at the house, he used to make chicken wraps for her and her whole team whenever she had tennis tournaments, he is constantly researching and buying her new musical equipment (when they're absolutely not made of money). When Mum had to leave her corporate office job and decided to pursue music full time, meaning they were a decent salary down, Dad didn't flinch.

I asked him about this recently and the fact that he wouldn't be able to shortly retire as he'd initially planned because he needed to stay working in order to support them both, and he said, "She should have been doing music a long time ago. It's worth it because look how happy she is."

I'm immensely proud to be his daughter. Don't tell him that though – if he asks, tell him this part of the book was horrible.

BECCI ABBOTT

The female parental unit

TWATTERY SCORE: "ANYWAYHERE'SWONDERWALL"/10

Now it's Mum's turn.

Job Title

- Freelance Composer / Part-Time Peripatetic Music Teacher / All-Round-Badass

Traits

- Sweet. Just so very sweet.
- Annoyingly talented pianist / guitarist / bassist / composer / any instrument the blasted woman picks up.
- Identical twin who, incidentally, is also an annoyingly talented musician. Bastards.
- Small beige lady of Sri Lankan heritage, seeing as how you asked.
- Cries easily.
- Very good with animals and children.
- Fucking loves Millets.
- Hair that simply cannot control itself.
- Looks disgustingly adorable in a onesie.
- Finds beauty in absolutely everything.
- Affectionate.
- Messy.
- Empathetic.
- Disorganised.
- Clever.
- Delicate and tactful (e.g. steering my 92-year-old-gran away from a bad decision whilst letting Gran think it was her idea).
- Tactile. She's the kind of person who will softly put her hand on your cheek or on top of your hand, sometimes randomly, to show you she loves you or she's proud of you.
- A great cuddler.

- Quick-witted.
- Competitive (yes I got this gene from both barrels so I had no chance. If we're playing a board game together you can bet your butt that the foulest language and verbal abuse will be coming from the little beige lady in the corner).
- Very good at sports and a right bastard in badminton or tennis when you give her the opportunity to smash a volley. Don't let her intriguing ethnic ambiguity and sweet little face fool you, Stan; she takes no prisoners.
- Proud of her extended family (including the Richings Lot). She'll gushingly support and love every single career or creative endeavour any of us undertake. She is so, so proud of everything we do, to the point that she's still the first person I call whenever I have any marginally positive news and absolutely beam with pride at her excitement like I'm still a toddler pulling at her hand and showing her the drawing I'd made.
- Will bend over backwards and drop everything if anyone needs anything from her.

Hobbies

- Being late to stuff.
- Playing in various bands.
- Running various choirs.
- Writing and recording beautiful music library tracks.

- Watching movies with you and asking you about the plot line mid-way through even though you've watched the exact same amount of the film as her.
- Tennis.
- Reading.
- Making, planning and following her daily schedule (this is her favourite and most time-consuming activity ever. It takes up most of her day).

Likes

- Going on walks (lol).
- Finding musicians in even the unlikeliest of places.
- Facebook videos of dads with cute babies.
- Skyping with her children and chatting for hours (what Dad calls "pointless chit-chat").
- Asking for stuff that isn't on the menu / a combination of starters instead of a main.
- Watching movies whilst cosy (blankets, hot chocolate, lots of cushions etc.).
- Dark chocolate.
- Herbal teas.
- Her little home studio.
- Food and movies about food.
- When Dad farts at funny moments.
- Self-help books.
- Ridiculously thin and pointless scarves.
- Making fun of Louis for being hairy.

- Music. Music gets to my mum in a big way and she passed down the trait of being truly touched and crying at anything beautiful we hear or see. Which is particularly annoying when you're in a family of talented musicians, so basically we cry a lot.

Dislikes

- Horror movies / gore.
- Being on time.
- Not being late.

Special Skills

- Bringing people together to play music.
- Finding musicians in even the unlikeliest of places. When left alone in public, my mum can spot a musician from a mile away. Even if they only occasionally play the flute in their spare time; even if they picked up a guitar once 15 years ago but then put it straight back down; even if the closest to music they've come is having a neighbour who owned a trombone – Mum will spot these people, bring out some secret part of them they didn't even know they had that wants nothing more than to make music with other people (surprising even to them), warmly encourage their music, invite them over to the house (sometimes with an accordion) and bring out the joy in their hearts.
- Making sticky toffee pudding.

- Ordering gifts for people and accidentally delivering it to herself instead of them.
- Making a home out of any environment, for anybody.
- Teaching music.
- Listening to a song for the first time and then being able to play it on the piano / guitar immediately.
- Winding Dad up.
- Swearing and calling you all sorts of awful names when you're beating her at online golf whilst also somehow still coming across as really sweet and innocent at the same time.
- Solid Daffy Duck impression.

Being the more sensitive and emotional parent, Mum probably struggled the most when I was in my especially difficult period. Her face swelled up due to stress and she used to cry a lot, storming out of the house in tears and going on furious, distraught drives to calm herself down. Both of us being emotional and unhappy (at this point she was working in a corporate office job when she should have been doing music) fuelled the fire and meant that we butted heads constantly. Where Dad could ignore my snide comments and general bitchiness, Mum couldn't. It hurt her feelings every time. She wanted to be close to me but I just wouldn't let her.

My Ma is a very special lady who loves hard and brings music to whatever she touches. She is patient and empathetic to a fault; to the point that she absorbs the pain or struggles of anyone she cares about and will do anything possible to help them at her own sacrifice (you can imagine how this was difficult for her when she was living with me as she was shouldering both her own and my anger). If we're all together, for example on our annual family holiday, Mum and Kath (her twin sister) will always be the last people to eat as they'll make sure everyone is fed first. They'll check everyone is being included in every game or quiz or sport so that the quieter ones aren't forgotten, they'll stay up late to clear up so everyone else doesn't have to, they'll run around making teas and coffees for all 20 of us (and by the time they're finished making the last drinks the first people will have finished theirs, so they just have to start the whole circuit again), they'll sit down with each person to ask them about their lives and they'll make sure everyone is feeling loved and included and full. They'll randomly tap your head when you walk past or grab your hand or pull you in for a hug, because they're just so happy to see you. When they're not in the foreground playing games and making music, they're in the background making sure that everything is special for everyone there. The pair of identical little sweethearts that we really rely on, even though they don't realise.

Mum feels everything and sees beauty in so much it overwhelms her sometimes. She brings family, joy and the gift of music to countless people and is an absolutely enormous figure (metaphorically speaking of course) in the local community, and in our family.

I genetically inherited Mum's tactileness (I'm a hugger), emotional oversensitivity, skin sensitivity, asthma, sarcasm, romanticism and huge love of people. I also got her messiness, forgetfulness, short attention span, fashion sense (or lack thereof), tasteful vocabulary and height restriction (with both of us towering at barely over 5 ft).

Mum and I call each other constantly about anything and everything. We can and do have multi-hour-long phone calls and Skype calls about nothing in particular and somehow manage to find conversation out of very little. We share books we love, media we enjoy, films we thought were interesting, Ted Talks, Facebook videos of hot dads with their cute babies (not that I'm broody but I make the exception when they're being lovingly held by a DILF).

Mum is so important to me I don't think I could really articulate it. I couldn't possibly quantify how close we are and how much I love that woman. We had our bad patch but really it was what we needed to figure out what we needed from each other and who we needed to be ourselves; I think that could be said for both of us. I'm so glad she's happy and that she's doing music full time as that lady was born to bring music into the world.

Oh, also, she loves Connaire. She really loves Connaire.

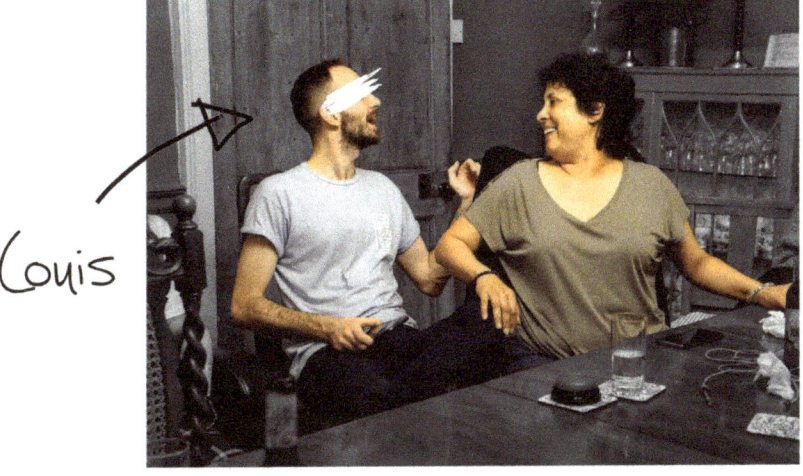

Acknowledgements

I can't believe I've actually written a book and get to do acknowledgements now; how cool is that? There's going to be a lot of heartfelt stuff in here so if that's not your bag, off you fuck x.

Obviously thank you to the big dogs: my mum and dad, for putting up with it all and still loving and supporting me regardless. For loving my friends as much (if not more) than me and for letting me turn out to be the fantastic person I am now. For filling my life with music in being able to hear Mum play guitar or in listening to Genesis with Dad, or the fact that you got me my start in working in the industry despite all the shit I put you through, which led to me meeting the love of my life. For the back-garden camping and the tennis and the curries and the Totopoly and the Blackadder and the Monster Truck Madness 2 and the pantomimes and the February holidays and the debates and the pies and the trying to bathe the cat when she's dirty and getting fucking mauled and the Devon trips and the train journeys and the sticky toffee puddings and the barbecues and the laughter. So much laughter.

To Jamie, get a haircut.

For Connaire, who shows me love far beyond my expectations and whom I really don't deserve but have anyway.

To my gran (who I get it all from and it's her fault really so blame her). You are incredibly beautiful and glamorous – even at 92 – leader of our tribe and we are so lucky to have you steering our ship. We love you beyond belief.

Thank you, Lukey, for being my editor, my writing companion, my poet, my fellow devil, my locksmith.

To Vicky, who I love more than Connaire. Thank you for supporting this ridiculous project and loving me no matter how annoying I am.

Thank you to Louise and Emily for your constant love, support and encouragement. You've given me the gift of having sisters.

To Ronnie and Ann-Marie for allowing me into your wonderful family. I hope I do you proud.

To the Richings lot: Vicky, Louis, Mike, Iz, Shawnee, Luke. You guys would have featured more heavily in the book if you'd been worse behaved, you boring arseholes – shame on you. Honestly – and Mike, I can feel you cringing from here at the soppiness that's coming but you're just going to have flipping well get over it because it's a-happenin' – one of the things in my life I'm most thankful for and most proud of is having you guys by my side as it reflects really well on me to have such awesome mates (as Mum likes to say). I remember when I was younger and always wanted to have a cool, close group of friends like they do on TV and aside from the 'cool' part, you gave me the gift of that.

You guys make my life worthwhile, even through the moments when I didn't really think it was. Thanks for the Christmas jumper parties, the leaving videos (oh yes you guys are getting a cringe list too, don't you think you wouldn't), the nights playing pool at The Chesnuts, the Tower Arms, mine and Micky's train trips down to Devon to see Granny and Grandad, the holidays: Bath, Bristol, Edinburgh, Lanzarote, Christchurch, Eastbourne, Cyprus, Brighton, Iceland, Scilly Isles, sky diving, bungee jumping, parties, birthdays, Slender Man, the arguments, the old friends, the open air cinema, the beer gardens, Liquid club in Windsor, the underpass, hanging at Iver station, the Alice in Wonderland treasure hunt round London, the drinks, making forts, the dogpiling, Reading Festival, the impression of a stag beetle (Shawnee), the ridiculous Snapchats, drinking red wine at pantomimes, all the train journeys, playing cards, the drunk facetimes with a mouthful of McDonald's fries (Louis), the Saturday morning hungover fry-ups, all the long sober Facetimes (Vicks), picnics by the lake, the sleepovers, being sat in Vicky's car for hours whilst smoking and talking about boys, Luke getting hit in the face by a crow on Logger's Leap at Thorpe Park when we were 10, the movie nights, every time we've ever sat on a sofa with our legs tangled together, every New Year's party, all of the generous lifts (so many lifts), the random bursting into song, the jams, the Eurovision extravaganzas, the hugs, the voice memos (Luke), the laughing fits (Iz), the drinking games, the pub crawls, the pure joy of every moment. We have our own shit, our own lives and other mates, but ultimately, we're always there and you guys are just my fucking world. I'm not crying, you're crying.

To Chris, Amy, Matt, Lou, Em and Josh. I have the best cousins ever, thank you for being my crew since day one.

To Kath, Tony, John, Sara, Amy I, Dave, Trev, Laura, Katya, Simon, Tracy, Ali & Gill. You are all incredibly wonderful, brilliant, talented and hilarious people and I regularly choose to spend my precious time with you voluntarily so that tells you everything really. Love you all immensely.

To the Moffs: Gawdy, Maz and Maryam. I've known Gawdy all my life and the overwhelming love that came into his life in the form of Maz and then later little Maryam has been magical to witness.

To Dave and Suzie, who are always there to care about us, protect us, advise us and also primarily to keep my dad in check. Suze read this whole book and was such a huge support when it was still a secret. Thank you for always caring about us so genuinely, no matter how far away you are. Also to Jadey and Rox, my other awesome cousins who I always looked up to when I was little and still do now. Rox, I'm so glad you moved to England and gave us the opportunity to be so close. I'm so proud to be part of the Abbott team fiercely led by Granny and Grandad.

To Julie. You housed and mothered a bunch of annoying teenagers. You made your home our home. You fixed our lives, listened to us, cared for us, fed us, laughed with us, smoked with us and really, really loved us. You were there throughout every step written about in this book whether mentioned or not and will be with us every step we'll take beyond these pages. This book ends before we lost you, but you'll never be forgotten, and you'll be forever loved.

To Libby who nursed us, James who cared for us, Nanu who gave me your last onion on my birthday, Carol who is where Vicky gets her sass and glamour from, Roger who's Vicky's twin in so many ways and Rae who is a gentle, kind rock whenever Vicks needs one. Thank you for being the literal and metaphorical blood that runs through my best friend's veins; you guys are the reason I love her (and you).

To Jean, Stephen, Jade, Jorgia, Harry, Skye, Leigh-Anne, Ron and George for welcoming me into your family and letting me be the number one girl to your number one boy.

To the McGuinnesses. I'll officially be one of you soon and I sincerely apologise in advance for tarnishing your good name.

To my incredibly talented saxophonist / clarinetist godmother Helen and your lovely husband Ian, for always thinking of me and being so very wonderful.

To Emma T, Yasmina, Jacob, Emma H, Michael, Connor, Christy, Laura, Jack, Fran, Paul, David, Hannah and Lucas, for letting me infiltrate your group with open arms and making me brave enough to move up and make Glasgow my home. Really quite fond of you guys.

To Ang, Louise, Caroline, Jennifer, Neil, Rose, Jenny, Val, Calli, Ash, Susana, Sharon and the rest of the MU family for just being so wonderful and supportive and making my working life a total joy.

To Nat and Shola, two of the strongest, coolest and most inspiring women I've met who guided me to become who I am now. No matter how long the time in between seeing each other, no matter what we always eventually end up back on Nat's sofa together, drinking wine and gossiping. I love you guys so much. To the rest of the OG Metropolis crew (my little Liam, Paul, Andy, Alex, Jed, Aaron, Nicky, Nina, Daryl, Ben, Sam, Xav, Nick, Simon, Pete, James, Felix, Wilbur, Humphrey) also for being by my side during some of the best years of my life.

To Jake, Emma, Matias, Fi and the rest of the Strongroom crew who saved me after I'd fallen.

To Karen, Kath and Rachel who let me ruin all their band practices when I was little.

To the Gorgeous Gibbsies, Sam and my darling Alf for looking after Mum and bringing her so much joy through your music and friendship. To Bert and Fred who used to babysit me and Mike when we were meant to be babysitting you.

To Rachael for keeping me from becoming spherical and being more of a therapist than a personal trainer.

SO YOUR CHILD IS A COMPLETE ARSEHOLE

To Steph, who set me up on a blind date with a gorgeous Scotsman and changed our lives forever.

To Nana, who raised five of the kindest, warmest, most talented and loving people in my life. Your softness and grace live on through them and their children (apart from Jamie).

For Grandad.

Julie

*Stan, I'm going to take this moment to talk about Julie. Don't worry, she's great, you'll love her.

People often talk about other people's mums saying they're like a second mum to them but I really can't overexaggerate how true this was for me in my case, nor how lucky I was to have her while we did. I'd go over to that little Tardis house on Wellesley Avenue with the porcelain sheep in the back garden if, say, I was crying because I'd had a fight with Mum / I was bored / I was invited for dinner / for a cup of tea with Julie whether Vicks was there or not. I'd knock on the door, hear Julie's familiar northern-accented voice shout "Password?" through the door to which I'd answer (no I'm not going to tell you the password, Stan, it's a secret) and I'd be greeted with a laugh and "Bex, give us a snog" then a smacking great kiss on the cheek, usually accompanied by the tapping of little paws as little Benji trotted up behind her. Julie would say this eeeeevery time I came in the house and I miss hearing that. *"Bex, give us a snog."* We sat around that bloody plastic multicoloured polka dot tablecloth in the kitchen more times than I could possibly count; Julie usually in her puffed gilet over a casual shirt and black leggings, plus her trademark trilby hat that she always looked effortlessly cool in. Each of us would be in our little usual spots: Me, Vicky, Libby (Vicky's sister) and Julie, or sometimes the rest of the Richings Lot too. There we would sit all together, smoking cigarettes, listening to music, drinking tea and just so very happy together. Julie would talk to me and the rest of the Richings Lot for hours; asking about our teenage lives (which must have been so mind-numbingly boring for her but she cared deeply and listened intently every single time) and our life goals and map out plans of how to achieve them. She also liked doing this last part to friends that we'd brought over to meet her for the first time and they always found it understandably intense. Other times she'd talk about her mad stories of all the trouble she's caused and the places she'd been. We'd watch Downton Abbey or Call The Midwife or Eurovision together (Julie had Eurovision score sheets she'd print out every year and took this very seriously; a tradition our group carries with us to this day except we've made it into a drinking game and get absolutely battered). Julie would make us Laksa Soup and Niçoise Salad and she showed me how to hang up socks on the washing line so they dry quicker. Sometimes we'd sit on the rocking chairs out the back with blankets wrapped around us watching the snow. We'd party with Julie's friends & family at the joint birthday garden parties she and Vicky would have (which were always pretty epic). I'd go over multiple times a week – sometimes daily – and most weekends and we'd just exist together.

Little bits of the house, my second house, will stick in my mind forever; the deep mustard-coloured sofas covered in throws & blankets, the huge peacock painting in the bathroom that eyed you up whenever you took a whizz, Vicky's first pair of obscenely tiny shoes that were on display behind the living room TV, the red kitchen chairs, the window frame of Vicky's ground floor bedroom that was coming off from the wall because of how often we used to sneak in and out late at night, the big Buddha painting that was in the spare bedroom upstairs (and now hangs behind me in my own spare bedroom in my little Glasgow flat where I'm writing this from right now), the box of Articulate in the cupboard under the stairs that we'd play all the time and would all desperately shotgun not being on Julie's team because she was rubbish at it, the picture of the woman eating a doughnut above the kitchen worktop, the pink 'fuck off, I'm smoking' mug.

For my 21st birthday Julie bought me an incredibly beautiful and delicate Tiffany & Co. bracelet with a tiny blue heart charm; one that she, Vicky, Libby and Freya (another wonderful family member) all had. I was officially part of the Hornby-Winfield Girls. Oftentimes Julie would sit me down very seriously and make sure I was still happy, still strong and always fearlessly independent. She'd grill our new boyfriends (at length) the first time she met them to make sure they respected us and give them 'the talk', telling them she'd knock them out if they didn't treat us right (she wouldn't – she was exceptionally tough but she wouldn't hurt a fly) and she raised her girls to be warriors, if a little terrifyingly headstrong when they want to be. Julie was a remarkable woman whose fascinating life deserves a book of its own one day (who knows, maybe that'll happen). Some people's loss leaves an unimaginable hole where laughter and colour once were. I'll truly love that mad woman forever.

SO YOUR CHILD IS A COMPLETE ARSEHOLE

SO YOUR CHILD IS A COMPLETE ARSEHOLE

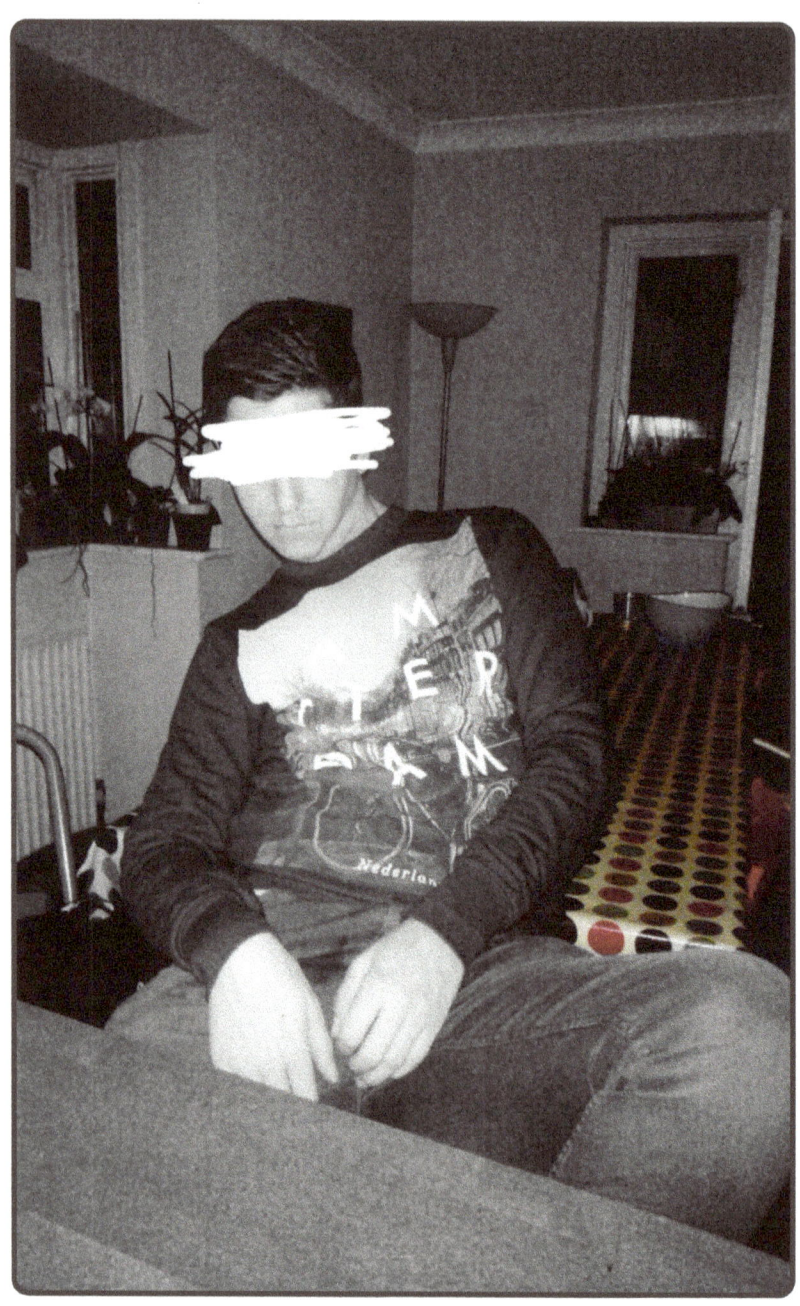

SO YOUR CHILD IS A COMPLETE ARSEHOLE

SO YOUR CHILD IS A COMPLETE ARSEHOLE

BECCI ABBOTT

About the Author

Becci is a passionate amateur juggler and yacht racer. She lives in Glasgow with her fiancé Connaire (who's wonderful despite being Scottish) and their 17 Italian greyhounds. When she's not flitting between her private islands or herding cattle, she can often be found in one of her dozens of Spanish allotments digging for buried treasure. She hopes one day to embark on her life's mission to enter the Guinness Book of World Records for clipping the most washing pegs onto the largest number of cabbages, so looks forward to inevitably releasing her forthcoming autobiography: 'Cabbage Clipper: A Hero's Journey'.

Lightning Source UK Ltd.
Milton Keynes UK
UKHW021313241220
375781UK00007B/121